A LAWYER'S GUIDE TO HEALING

"Don Carroll, a national leader in the lawyer assistance community and a prolific writer, has clearly outdone himself in *A Lawyer's Guide to Healing*. Drawing on his rich professional and personal experience, Don manages to combine the latest data on addiction, depression, and other problems besetting altogether too many lawyers with stories of overcomers and practical words of encouragement which are nothing short of inspiring. Any lawyer or judge struggling with these issues—or assisting those who are—must read this wise and instructive book."

—JUDGE CARL HORN III
author of Fourth Circuit Criminal Handbook *and*
LawyerLife: Finding a Life and a Higher Calling in the Practice of Law

"This is a book about healing for lawyers who may not know they need help or healing. As a lawyer speaking to other lawyers, Don Carroll provides a simple, straightforward, and very wise primer about addiction. He offers a handbook of philosophy, science, and psychology, along with plenty of direct advice to help his colleagues recognize their self-deception and face themselves. Best of all, he offers these radical suggestions for change with an attitude of great hope."

—STEPHANIE BROWN, PH.D.
author of A Place Called Self: Women, Sobriety, and Radical Transformation
and director of the Addictions Institute, Menlo Park, California

"Don speaks with the voice of one who knows the processes which lead to the 'dark night of the soul,' as well as the pathways out of that dark night to transformation, recovery, and healing. This book is a gift of guidance and inspiration to lawyers seeking healing from addiction and depression and to those offering help."

—AL J. MOONEY, M.D.
coauthor of The Recovery Book

"This book represents a unique resource for attorneys struggling with alcoholism and substance abuse, as well as the medical professionals and lawyer assistance volunteers and personnel who work with them. Don Carroll provides a wealth of information regarding impairment and recovery, while never losing sight of the human side of the equation. The book presents the pain of addiction and the joy of recovery, together with the information needed to assist suffering legal professionals."

—MICHAEL COHEN
*executive director of Florida Lawyers Assistance, Inc., and member of the
Florida Bar Standing Committee on Professionalism*

A LAWYER'S GUIDE TO HEALING

Solutions for Addiction and Depression

Don Carroll, J.D.

HAZELDEN

Hazelden
Center City, Minnesota 55012-0176

1-800-328-0094
1-651-213-4590 (Fax)
www.hazelden.org

ISBN-13: 978-1-59285-379-3
ISBN-10: 1-59285-379-X

10 09 08 07 06   6 5 4 3 2 1

Cover design by David Spohn
Interior design by Rachel Holscher
Typesetting by Prism Publishing Center

Editor's note

This publication is designed to provide accurate information in regard to the subject matter covered. It is sold with the understanding that the publisher and author are not engaged in rendering psychological, financial, legal, or other professional services. If expert counseling is needed, the services of a competent professional should be sought.

To protect the anonymity of author conversations with clients, pseudonyms have been used to represent actual clients. No real client of a Lawyer Assistance Program is referred to by name in this book.

To the PALS *and* FRIENDS *volunteers*
of the North Carolina Lawyer Assistance Program

Contents

Section 1: Understanding Alcoholism and Other Addictions

Section 2: Understanding Depression

Section 3: Understanding the Solutions

Foreword

DON CARROLL, director of the North Carolina Lawyer Assistance Program (NC-LAP), has collected knowledge about addiction and recovery during his many years of training and on-the-job experience helping addicted and depressed lawyers in North Carolina. His commitment to and care for troubled lawyers has helped save lives and salvage careers, law practices, and relationships. Don has gathered wisdom about the insidious diseases of addiction and depression and the hope of recovery through countless encounters with lawyers who have hit bottom and in fellowship with the many lawyers who offer a hand-up of mutual support and shared learning about the ways of healthy living.

Don speaks with the voice of one who knows the processes that lead to the "dark night of the soul," as well as the pathways out of that dark night to transformation, recovery, and healing. This book is a gift of guidance and inspiration to lawyers seeking healing from addiction and depression, and to those offering help.

On behalf of the NC-LAP and the North Carolina State Bar, I am grateful to Don for his wise and steady service to our program. He has done it all: interventions, arranging for care and aftercare, organizing and leading groups, speaking and writing for the NC-LAP, arranging for and leading educational and training programs for volunteers, and the thankless but necessary administrative work to keep it all going. I am thankful for his leadership in the cause of helping recovering lawyers through the American Bar Association's Commission on Lawyer Assistance Programs (CoLAP). Don has often been a speaker at and organizer of CoLAP events, and has done much to advance the cause of helping recovering lawyers across the footprint of the CoLAP, which includes the United States and Canada.

I am honored to call Don my friend and can attest to his good company in travel, in the fellowship of working for the well-being of our brother and sister lawyers, and in the occasional pursuit of fish with a fly rod.

Ed Hinson
North Carolina State Bar councilor
Former chair, North Carolina
    Lawyer Assistance Program board

Foreword

EVERY NOW AND THEN a published work offers a tangible contribution to the betterment of our society. In this book on alcoholism and addiction, Don Carroll has thoroughly addressed a complex yet incredibly important subject. Fortunately, many people will benefit from his decision to preserve these insights under a single cover. At first glance, the legal profession would appear to be a peripheral audience for education about our country's number one unmet health need, but through Mr. Carroll's influence, the North Carolina State Bar has positively impacted recovery every bit as much as medical and psychiatric specialists have done. The North Carolina Lawyer Assistance Program has saved countless lives and families. More importantly, however, it has promoted an attitude and infrastructure with more effective, humane, and efficient solutions for addiction treatment than we have previously seen. By means of this publication, Mr. Carroll affords others beyond North Carolina a similar opportunity to address addiction issues.

This text is comprehensive and covers alcoholism, addiction, and recovery. Sections devoted to mental problems other than addiction expand the scope of conditions ameliorated by the lawyer assistance effort.

The book's readability allows the novice to gain an accurate and deep understanding of addiction and recovery. At the same time, the material presented here creates a detailed, cohesive paradigm of this illness, its treatment, and the recovery process that will be useful to the expert. The publication blends scientific evidence, psychological principles, and spiritual concepts. It also fully embraces the undeniable effectiveness of Alcoholics Anonymous, Al-Anon, and other mutual support fellowships. The material motivates the reader toward constructive involvement. Enlightenment from this publication has the great potential to remove the stigma contributing to the bondage of alcoholics in the world's freest country.

Mr. Carroll is providing real leadership by making this information available to those outside North Carolina. It is also appropriate that those who truly value the freedom our society represents build on this endeavor, to transform the affliction of addictive disease into a stepping-stone to the wonderful gift of recovery.

Al J. Mooney, M.D.
Coauthor, *The Recovery Handbook*

Acknowledgments

THREE GROUPS OF PEOPLE and several organizations are the reason you have this book in your hands. The first group is the North Carolina lawyers and judges whom I have been privileged to work with over the past ten-plus years as director of the North Carolina Lawyer Assistance Program (NC-LAP). Because of this group's courage in facing issues of addiction and depression, my understanding of these disorders has moved beyond theory to the real world mysteries of surrender, willingness, perseverance, and that open-heartedness of one person unselfishly helping another that we lump into that huge word "love." I am grateful to each lawyer whose personal struggle has contributed to the understanding and insights that are shared with the reader. That said, no client of the NC-LAP is referred to either in whole or in any recognizable part in this book.

This is a grassroots book and I give special thanks for their support of this book to my own local Bar in Charlotte, North Carolina (the Mecklenburg County Bar) as well as the Lawyer Support Committee of that Bar and the Mecklenburg Bar Foundation. I especially thank Shirley Fulton, Mecklenburg County Bar president; Marion Cowell, Mecklenburg Bar Foundation president; Nancy Roberson, Bar director; Tom Dickinson, chair of the Lawyer Support Committee; and all committee members whose processing with committee member Cassandra Tydings developed the title for the book.

I have been a member of the American Bar Association since 1975. After becoming the director of the NC-LAP, I have participated in the activities of the American Bar Association's Commission on Lawyer Assistance Programs (CoLAP). I have been privileged to serve on the commission for three years. My participation in the CoLAP has introduced me to the directors of Lawyer Assistance Programs (LAPs) across the country. I owe all of my peer directors a huge debt, but particularly I owe a debt of gratitude, for the longstanding sharing of their experience and wisdom, to Michael Cohen of Florida, Bill Kane of New Jersey, Bonnie Waters of Massachusetts, Bill Leary of Louisiana, Mike Sweeney of Oregon, and Barbara Harper of Washington. Each has been involved in LAP work longer than I have, and each has unstintingly given freely of their time and experience to help other LAP directors. This book is a beneficiary of their giving.

In addition to the individual contributions of many LAP directors, the CoLAP's commitment to this book has helped make its publication possible, and I am deeply grateful to the CoLAP and its current chair, Richard A. Soden, for this support.

I am indebted to the LAP directors from Virginia, Tennessee, and South Carolina, who are, respectively, Susan Pauley (former director), Robert Albury, and Robert Turnbull, with whom North Carolina has over the past several years jointly put on a Step study retreat for lawyers in recovery. The retreats and the friendships of these directors has been a sustaining influence for me and helped make possible the work you have in your hands.

The third group of people that made this book possible is the past presidents of the North Carolina State Bar under whom I have served, my LAP board chairs and LAP board members, the executive director of the State Bar, my assistant director and the LAP staff, and, most importantly, all of the PALS and FRIENDS volunteers who have given of themselves to help others. Tom Lunsford, the executive director of the North Carolina State Bar, has always been there to support the LAP and to give the benefit of his wisdom on issues that emerged from time to time beyond our everyday work. Each Bar president under whom I have served has been supportive, and I thank them all. Bob Sink must be mentioned by name as he was the thoughtful Bar president who took our program "broad brush." I owe a debt of gratitude to the Bar's Publication Committee for the many LAP columns that have been published in the *North Carolina State Bar Journal* and to the *Campbell Law Observer* for the many LAP columns published there. Many of these formed the basis for the material appearing in this book. For his critique of these articles, and his care and commas, I need to thank Ed Ward.

In fact, my job would today seem impossible if not for the caring and wonderful assistance of Ed Ward, assistant LAP director; Towanda Garner, LAP Piedmont coordinator; LAP assistant Betty Whitley; and my former assistant, Renae Powers—thank you for your hard work each day. Each LAP board chair has made special contributions to me and LAP. I particularly would like to thank Judge Phil Howerton, Steve Philo, Dan Dean, Ed Hinson, Sara Davis, and Victor Boone for their strong and committed leadership of the LAP board. I would also like to thank Calvin Murphy for his assistance in seeing that this book was printed and made available in North Carolina while he was president of the North Carolina State Bar.

While they contributed to none of its deficiencies, I owe special thanks to those who read the manuscript and contributed comments and good direction, including Dr. Al Mooney, Michael Cohen, Carollee Cameron, Reita Pendry, CoLAP chair Richard A. Soden, CoLAP editorial chair Hugh Grady, and especially to CoLAP executive administrator Donna Spilis, for her dedication and enthusiasm for this project. Special thanks also to Hazelden's Jodie Carter, Richard Solly, Ann Standing, and Nick Motu for the enthusiasm and expertise they have given to this project.

Introduction

This book is for lawyers who find law challenging, frustrating, or stressful—either a dream that must be pursued or a vision that cannot be ignored. This book offers insight into the addictive and emotional problems lawyers face and a special understanding of how we, as lawyers, become susceptible, get sick, and can seek help and recover.

Much of the information in this book about the nature of addictive disease and depression is not new. What is different is that this book places the best contemporary understanding of these issues into the context of the real-world problems of lawyering. If there is a repeated warning or a recurring theme in the book, it is to be wary of how the fast-paced, demanding life of a lawyer can subtly bring a kind of emotional isolation that is the seedbed for disease and dysfunction. If there is a repetitious positive refrain, it is the powerful hope that lies in solutions that break down this isolation.

Just as being a lawyer brings special health risks to each of us who choose the profession, the career also brings certain opportunities for healing that are not found elsewhere. Despite the years of bad jokes and press, we work in a profession that is about more than just making a living and aspires to things much larger than our own individual career goals. By virtue of that professionalism, being a lawyer offers an opportunity for healing not found elsewhere.

The gateways to healing are the Lawyer Assistance Programs that exist in almost every state in the country. While the American Bar Association's Commission on Lawyer Assistance Programs (CoLAP) provides guidance and leadership, each separate program is the simple result of more than one lawyer caring about what is happening to another brother or sister lawyer. Yes, it is a tough, competitive, wounding profession, but we look after our wounded. This book salutes that fact. You are invited to discover in these pages not only how to better look after yourself but also how to better understand and help those in our profession who need to heal.

Understanding Alcoholism and Other Addictions

CHAPTER ONE

Personality, Environment, and Addiction
Why Lawyers Use Alcohol and Other Drugs

IF I HAD TO PICK the most common malady affecting lawyers, it would be alcoholism. Many lawyers use alcohol to self-medicate against career stress and to cope with their own challenging personality traits, which can include perfectionism, the need to control, and grandiosity. No other coping mechanism seems to "fit" while offering a way to handle the often stressful and demanding conditions under which law is practiced.

Lawyers often have incredibly high expectations of themselves and what they should accomplish on behalf of their clients. A lawyer is constantly looking for others to make a mistake, while at the same time he or she feels that others are diligently looking for him or her to slip. Together, these thoughts and attitudes dramatically increase a lawyer's level of stress. Some lawyers addicted to alcohol or other drugs have a very hard time losing and are overly sensitive, which can be a great source of stress and resentment.

In response to stress, many lawyers learn to cut off their emotions so they don't have to deal with them. These emotions are then repressed in the psyche. Whether or not lawyers are conscious of these unwanted emotions, they are still there. In fact, the more repressed the unwanted emotions are, the stronger the unconscious need to seek another way of feeling.

One question I am often asked when meeting with local Bar organizations is "Are lawyers really more likely than the general population to become addicted to alcohol or other drugs?" My answer, unfortunately, is "Yes." In 2002, the Substance Abuse and Mental Health Services Administration (SAMHSA) estimated that 9.4 percent of Americans age twelve and older could be generally classified as substance abusers or substance dependent. According to reports by the American Bar Association (ABA), the corresponding estimate for lawyers is between 15 and 18 percent—nearly double the number of the general population.[1]

Many lawyers learn from their first drink that it is much easier to deal with stress and avoid uncomfortable emotional feelings by using alcohol as a damper. This is because alcohol is a central nervous system depressant, but its initial effect is to elevate the mood and to release tension. Eventually, for many lawyers, the emotional burden of resentment and anger can only be relieved by having a drink at the end of the day—and over time the thought of having a drink becomes an obsession.

In my experience, perfectionism and a need to control are two key personality traits that serve lawyers well in their careers, but these characteristics also leave lawyers at a high risk for substance abuse. Many lawyers have personality traits that could be described as those of "the natural philosopher." These traits include the need to control by understanding and a natural curiosity. One of my best law professors saw law as a service profession. He always said that it wasn't the lawyer who knew the law best, but the lawyer who knew more of the facts of the case that would ultimately prevail. Most lawyers possess this inherent yearning to understand.

In general, it may be said that it is the nature of the alcoholic or addict's ego to try to reach beyond its bounds in order to control other people, places, and things. In our society, such grandiosity can promote a lawyer in his or her accomplishments, but it also can create a lot of frustration, which the lawyer may try to soothe with alcohol or other drugs. Addicted lawyers often don't see themselves as having these controlling characteristics. This is because the ability to see their life objectively is impaired by the disease of addiction.

Many lawyers are interested in finding a connection to deep meaning in their lives. Dr. Dwayne Book, an addiction psychiatrist, defines spirituality as the process of connection—connection to self, to others, and to something beyond and greater than the self. Dr. Carl Jung in his famous letter to Bill Wilson, one of the founders of Alcoholics Anonymous (AA), noted that the alcoholic is engaged in a misplaced effort to find that spiritual connection from a bottle of spirits when he or she really is longing for a spiritual connection to life. Most lawyers I know would like to have a connection to something that gives life vitality and real meaning. Alcohol and other drugs offer the lure of providing that connection, albeit a lure that becomes more and more illusory, until eventually, these substances block the addict completely.

CHAPTER TWO

The Addictive Personality

Is There a Link between Personality and Addiction?

DOES THE PRACTICE OF LAW draw to it particular personality types that may be more prone to addiction, both chemical (alcohol and other drugs) and nonchemical (sex, food, gambling, and so on)? In talking about personality types, it is important to understand that we all develop our own way of existing in and interacting with the external world. These personality traits can lead us into careers that offer a venue where we can maximize our strengths. For example, certain personalities tend to be drawn to careers as jet pilots, others to nursing or teaching, and still others are drawn to the practice of law.[1]

I would like to focus on two particular personality types that are drawn to law and look at the nature of these types to ascertain their susceptibility to addiction. I call these two personality types the "romantic-idealist personality" and the "judge personality."

First I will cover the romantic-idealist personality. Lawyers are often drawn to the legal profession because of a longing to bring about justice and to move closer to an ideal world. As these lawyers grow, they develop a personal vision of how life ought to be. This ideal vision incorporates family beliefs as well as cultural and religious values. Developing this personal vision is part of maturing as an individual. As the psyche develops, most people are able to come to terms with the fact that their ideal vision might not always be possible in the real world.

For the romantic-idealist, the desire to live in this ideal world can take over his or her life, reducing the person's ordinary existence to the futility of insatiable longing to correct the world, piece by piece. When this occurs, the romanticized ideal has become an addiction. This romantic aspect is not just a powerful personal aspect of the psyche, but it is also a strong force in our culture. In American culture, we romanticize the lives of celebrities and athletes. What happens to young celebrities or athletes with romantic ideals also can happen to young lawyers in their attitude about the profession. If a lawyer's personality is dominated by an overly rigid, idealistic view of what the law can achieve, he or she inevitably becomes frustrated with his or her career as a lawyer because the longed-for ideal is never achieved. When this happens, romanticism degenerates into a cynical, life-denying resentment. The addictive romantic then refuses to live in the tension of the real human world and may find escape in chemical or other addictive behaviors.

The romantic-idealist lawyer tends to have a very acute sensitive feeling for life. He or she often feels the weight of injustice in a profound way. These wonderful, caring characteristics become addictive when the romantic-idealist becomes inflated (feels that he or she *brings* justice or is personally responsible for what happens to a client). Then the desire to achieve the ideal becomes obsessive-compulsive. Inevitably, this overly responsible side of the personality—this ideal notion of who one is as a lawyer—must have some compensation; it must be freed in some way.

Drinking enables the romantic idealist to forget the burdens, tensions, and responsibilities he or she has taken on in this idealistic quest. Not only does drinking provide this instinctual relief, it also, at least initially, provides the feeling of ecstasy, union, and completion—the hoped-for fulfillment that seems to lie behind the idealistic drive.

Lawyers may not be able to create justice in their day-to-day practice, but at least they can achieve union with the divine ideal for a few fleeting moments in the euphoria of alcohol or other drugs. Using these substances provides an escape from the cynicism and resentment that represent the romantic's acute disappointment with life. Life is then bearable only through the regular use of these mood-altering chemicals.

The irony then is that this lawyer's most positive aspect—the drive to create good and to make things better—is often felt as a desire to perform perfectly. This quest for perfection, unless transformed, will set him or her up for addiction. The addiction of the romantic-idealist is really an expression of the desire for divine justice. Only when this desire is understood symbolically—when the addicted person understands his or her own powerlessness in achieving this goal—can the addiction be overcome.

Addicts, in giving themselves over to alcohol, other drugs, power, or idealism, are trying to escape the conflicts and tensions of life. They are unable to live in the tension, the paradox of opposites that is the human condition. The addict's tendency is to live in the extremes: either idealism and perfection, or despair and cynicism. When the romantic is able to endure the tension of striving for ideals without using substances, then he or she will make an enormously creative and important contribution to the profession of law.

Let's look next at another personality type, that of the judge. One of the most effective portraits of the judge-type personality is found in Leo Tolstoy's novel *The Death of Ivan Ilyich.* The story of Ilyich illustrates a rigid, self-justifying personality who, when confronted with a trauma in his own life, hopes that the pressures and routines of going to court will destroy his own personal pain. Ilyich struggles mightily to deny and to protest his "sickness." Transformation in the story comes when Ilyich descends into the abyss of his own suffering, experiences his own powerlessness and vulnerability, and surrenders to the mystery of his suffering as a human being. In this way, he lets go of the rigid internal judge that controls his personality.

We see a similar judge figure in Albert Camus' *The Fall.* In this story we encounter the judge, Jean-Baptiste Clamence, who wants to look good and be above it all. He strives for a perfect personality, a proper appearance, and a charming manner, all of which tend to hide his arrogance and his judgment of others, particularly women, as inferior. In the story, Clamence happens to pass by a woman who appears to be committing suicide by drowning. Hurrying on in a self-righteous manner, Clamence rejects the opportunity to assist her, to seek to prevent her suicide. As time passes he becomes haunted by his failure to reach out to help another human being. He strives to avoid judgment of himself by judging others first—avoiding his own guilt by trying to make others feel more guilty.

Clamence's story has a parallel among alcoholics and other addicts who die from the disease of addiction. Most alcoholics and addicts rationally understand that they are drinking or using themselves to death. They are unable to give up their rigid control, to have hope, and to accept the risk that help must come from outside of themselves. Even though an addict's life is obviously out of control, the rigid inability to accept this and give up the illusion of personal control makes death from addiction inevitable, presenting a tragic end like Clamence's.

The judge in Camus' novel was never able to surrender to his own vulnerability and powerlessness. Ilyich's surrender to his equitable aspect (to use the metaphor of our profession) accounts for his transformation and what allows for the legal and equitable qualities in him to come to exist in a healthy pattern.

Dr. Ted Clark, one of North Carolina's pioneers in treating chemical dependency, believes, "If there is any hallmark of the addictive personality, it is in the area of doing things to excess or not at all." In the judge type of addictive personality, the legal qualities of judging are not informed by equitable qualities of humanness. Objectivity, discrimination, and critical perception are all wonderful and necessary qualities for a judge, but these may form a rigid, controlling personality when the individual lacks the normal counterbalancing equitable qualities of vulnerability and powerlessness.

In the practice of law and in the task of judgment, being able to ascertain the facts of a case are extremely important, but in making those judgments, equitable aspects are necessary for true justice to be achieved. This process can perhaps best be seen in the central image of our profession: Athena, the goddess of justice. Athena is often depicted as a statue of a seated woman in a hall of justice or as a statue atop a courthouse. In her right hand she holds a large unsheathed sword. This sword symbolizes the quality of differentiation, of being able to cut away fiction from fact. In her left hand she holds the scales of justice, two pans connected by a horizontal rod. This imagery suggests openness to the duality of the human condition, both spiritual and material existence.

This symbol of the legal profession also suggests the qualities necessary for the judge-dominated addictive personality to be transformed. For wholeness of personality, as well as for justice to be served, Athena suggests the way out. Addiction in the judge-dominated personality is manifest in the need to control—to control others and to control all aspects of life. The image of the naked sword can be seen as representing the way to cut through denial, the illusion of control, and the false images given by addiction. The legal weapon of discrimination is needed to meet life responsibly, and the sword implies the necessity of sacrifice for this to occur. Indeed, for recovery to occur, the addict must sacrifice dependency on the mood-altering substance that controls his or her life.

The task for us, as lawyers, is to try to relate to the personality of the judge within us in a way that prevents our internal judge from being a tyrant. As a profession, lawyers are no doubt drawn from the judging personality type more strongly than other groups. The healthy part of this judging aspect is central to the greatness of the legal profession, but its dominance of the personality is also an open door to addiction, whether nonchemical addictive behavior such as gambling, sex, or excessive work, or a chemically based addictive behavior such as alcohol, amphetamine, or cocaine use.

The key to sobriety and health is to balance these legal and equitable qualities and to be willing to surrender to the universal human condition. Lawyers who have a romantic-idealist or judging personality should be proud of the positive aspects of these personality types and truly appreciate the gifts contained in them. At the same time, they should be aware that these ways of being in the world could make them more susceptible to an addictive disease.

Just as the disease of addiction is common among lawyers, so is recovery. One of the profound changes recovery can bring is that personal selfish desires are placed in a more subservient role. The addict begins to live life in a manner in which thoughts are centered not on what we can *get* out of life, but on what we can *give* to others.

CHAPTER THREE

Understanding Alcoholism

How Alcoholism Manifests in Various Forms

IN 1960, E. M. JELLINEK published the seminal book *The Disease Concept of Alcoholism.* In this book, Jellinek presented and summarized what was known at that time about alcoholism. He found that there were five subtypes of alcoholics. Since the publication of Jellinek's book, there have been numerous efforts to explore and research the seemingly infinite variations of the disease, but even after more than forty years, Jellinek's subtypes remain critical to our understanding of alcoholism.

Modern medicine was founded on the notion that illness is simply a biological phenomenon. Initially, when researchers began looking at alcoholism, they worked to isolate the biological components in order to "prove" addiction was a disease. These biological aspects, particularly the idea of genetic predisposition to acquire the disease and what happens in the brain when the disease is active, have now been explored through research, though much is yet to be learned.

More and more medical doctors are realizing that diseases have not only biological, but also social, psychological, and spiritual aspects. While there are biological, psychological, social, and spiritual issues with alcoholism and other addictions, so are there with heart disease, cancer, and other diseases. It is well known that alcoholics have a greater chance of getting better with an accepting peer support group such as Alcoholics Anonymous (AA). The same is true of cancer patients. Alcoholics have a greater chance of recovering if they make spiritual practices—such as prayer and meditation—a daily part of their lives. The same is true for those who suffer from other diseases such as multiple sclerosis. Much of the old-fashioned biology-based Western medicine overlooks beneficial approaches based in psychology and spirituality.

The reality is that all diseases have biological, social, psychological, and spiritual aspects. One of the great contributions of alcoholism treatment to the world of disease treatment has been the insistence on recognizing the multi-factored aspects of the disease of chemical addiction. This multifaceted nature must be borne in mind when we look at the different subtypes of alcoholics and the approach to the treatment of addiction as a whole.

Jellinek used Greek letters to label the various subtypes of alcoholics, and I have elaborated his definitions in terms of the type of lawyer who fits into each category.

I have found that "alpha" alcoholic lawyers are psychologically dependent on alcohol but do not yet have physical dependence or physiological damage. These are lawyers who report consuming three to five alcoholic drinks almost every day but do not yet have physical dependence on alcohol. These lawyers often feel alcohol is not a problem for them since they feel they can quit without experiencing withdrawal. In other words, their physical body does not demonstrate the overt physiological signs of addiction. Without overt physical signs, these lawyers will often ignore the addiction.

As humans, we experience our emotional well-being through our moods. Our moods serve as lights on an instrument panel that tell us that we need to respond to events in our life. When a light comes on—whether it signals anger, grief, or joy—a healthy response is to take action based on both the emotion and the external event that precipitated the emotion. I have found that alpha lawyers tend to respond to these emotional signals by consuming alcohol. They use alcohol to alter their mood rather than address the emotional issue directly. Out of touch with true emotional experience, the alpha alcoholic lawyer will tend to be overly sensitive, or overly insensitive and rageful, or both.

It is my experience that "beta" alcoholic lawyers are socially heavy drinkers who are not physically addicted to the drug, but share the emotional dependency found in the alpha lawyer. However, unlike the alpha lawyers, beta lawyers suffer alcohol-related physical health problems. They seem to have a physiological predisposition that allows them to tolerate a substantial amount of alcohol without actually getting physically dependent, but the result of their ability to drink heavily is secondary damage to an organ (such as the liver) that may itself cause another disease. Beta lawyers may not drink a lot during the week, but during the weekend they are red-faced party animals. Because of their resistance to physical dependence, they manifest a good bit of control and are able to subject their bodies to a level of abuse that it eventually cannot withstand. Beta alcoholics are often psychologically dependent and have arrested emotional development.

I find that "gamma" alcoholic lawyers are both physically and psychologically dependent on alcohol. Whether this physical dependency has arisen from just a limited use of alcohol or as a progression from the alpha or beta stages over a period of years, the gamma alcoholic lawyer feels that he or she *must* use alcohol. The gamma lawyer's fear is that he or she might not have alcohol available. This lawyer is unwilling to tolerate the physical discomfort and anxiety he or she feels if there is not continual alcohol in the body. Unless the gamma alcoholic's course is arrested by treatment and sobriety, his or her condition will progressively get worse, and at some point there will be organ-related damage or death. The gamma lawyer has to schedule his or her whole life around alcohol in order to feel he or she can survive. The gamma lawyer does not drink just to escape challenging emotions, he or she drinks to survive. Control over alcohol use is progressively lost, and with loss of control this lawyer increasingly tends to isolate. Gamma lawyers are prone to isolate for days at a time. In later stages, they will often drink during the day and may show up in court or at a client conference drunk.

My experience shows that the "delta" alcoholic lawyer is someone who is physically and psychologically dependent on alcohol, but unlike the gamma lawyer who is unable to control the amount of his or her alcohol intake, the delta lawyer is able to maintain the same level of alcohol intake day after day. Delta lawyers are maintenance drinkers who consume alcohol to feel okay, but they are able to control their level of input. Because of their feeling of control, they are often the most strident to assert that they have no problem with alcohol. Essentially, their fate is similar to the gamma alcoholic, but because they control their intake, they may be able to go much longer without secondary organ damage.

The psychological damage to delta lawyers is as great as any group, and psychological damage is perhaps most severe to those around them.

This is because of the insidious "controlled" nature, and because the high level of control may prevent behavioral problems from occurring that often lead to help. This lawyer drinks every day, often immediately after returning home from work, and his or her marriage or significant relationship may be emotionally dead. The delta lawyer gradually develops a harsher and harsher view of life, believing that others don't work as hard as he or she does. Because the delta lawyer keeps a tenaciously rigid grip on life, he or she can be critical of others who are carefree or compassionate.

I find the "epsilon" alcoholic lawyer to be a periodic alcoholic. There is some belief that all alcohol and other drug users have a tendency to develop their own cycle of use. In the epsilon lawyer the cycle is characterized by binges that occur weeks or months apart. The binges can be so excessive, the epsilon alcoholic's behavior may get him or her into trouble and he or she may end up in treatment. The epsilon lawyer, having mastered a moderate amount of willful control, may go without using alcohol for six months up to two years or more, but ultimately he or she suffers from chronic relapses. Unless treated, this lawyer stuffs down the dynamics of the disease so that drinking eruptions worsen.

One of the hallmarks of recovery is an increasing ability to be honest. It is important to apply this honesty to what we say to others about the disease of addiction. Some would argue that only the gamma, delta, and epsilon alcoholics truly have the disease. It is my belief that disease is not a biological concept as much as it is a broader concept defined by pain and suffering. The emotional pain of alcoholism and other drug addictions can be severe. According to the American Foundation for Suicide Prevention, one out of every four successful suicides is the result of alcoholism.

While it is important to continue to search for ways in which treatment can be designed to meet the specific needs of each subtype, the most effective treatment programs available are those programs that turn out good members. Whether an individual is an alpha, beta, gamma, delta, or epsilon alcoholic, the program can arrest the biological injury caused by alcoholism; it can alleviate the social and psychological pain caused by alcoholism and provide a sense of equanimity and internal serenity.

CHAPTER FOUR

The Science of Addiction

What Research Reveals about the Causes of Alcohol and Drug Addiction

IN AN EFFORT to increase our understanding of alcoholism and develop more effective treatment programs, researchers are studying the development of the disease among people in various age groups by using longitudinal studies that extend as long as fifty years. This is important because alcohol is a disease that changes in its severity and manifestation over time. The active alcoholic personality lies, evades, and dissembles in whatever fashion is necessary to support the internal illusion that his or her drinking is not a problem. These characteristics are sociopathic in nature and inevitably erode professional trust.

Longitudinal research has shown that alcoholism can develop slowly over a person's life and can occur in people of all ages. There is no one cause of alcoholism, but heredity, culture, economics, and the environment all contribute to its development. Alcohol can have long-term effects on the central nervous system that can gradually change the alcoholic's personality.

Dr. George E. Vaillant, author of *The Natural History of Alcoholism*, professor of psychiatry at Harvard Medical School, and director of the Study of Adult Development at Harvard University Health Services, has asked some very important questions about alcoholism:

- Is alcoholism an independent disease or the symptom of an underlying disorder?
- Do certain characteristics distinguish people who eventually become alcoholics from those who do not?

• Is alcoholism always a progressive disorder?
• How does alcoholism treatment or participation in self-help
  groups, such as AA, influence the disease process?
• Is abstinence the only reasonable treatment goal, or can alcoholics safely return to social drinking?

For his investigation, Dr. Vaillant chose two unique study samples.
The first, called the "College" sample, consists of 268 male participants
recruited from the sophomore classes at Harvard University between
1939 and 1944. Vaillant has been following and interviewing these participants every year or every other year. The "Core City" sample is a
group of 456 men selected between 1940 and 1944 from Boston inner-
city schools. These men were interviewed extensively before 1974 and
every two years since 1974. This study has continued for the natural
lives of the participants.

By following the drinking patterns and alcohol-related medical problems of these two groups of men, Vaillant was able to reach the following conclusions:

1. *Psychiatric disorders, or the symptoms of psychiatric disorders,
   develop as a consequence of alcoholism, not the other way
   around.* In most of the study participants who became alcoholics, alcoholism was clearly the first and primary disease
   and other psychiatric conditions were secondary. The only
   exception was that the prior existence of a sociopathic personality produced a higher risk that alcoholism could develop later.

2. *Genetics and cultural background increase the risk of alcoholism.* This study showed that the disease of alcoholism can
   be passed on from one generation to the next (particularly in
   sons of alcoholic fathers). In the College sample, 26 percent
   of the men with alcoholic relatives became alcoholics, as opposed to 9 percent of the men who did not have alcoholism
   in their families. In the Core City sample, 34 percent of the
   men with alcoholic relatives became alcoholics and 10 percent
   of the men who did not have alcoholism in their families
   did. Cultural background also appears to affect susceptibility

to addiction. The Core City sample was very useful because it represented a variety of ethnic backgrounds including Irish, Polish, Russian, English, Italian, French Canadian, Anglo Canadian, and other Northern and Southern Europeans. Strikingly, alcoholism was five times less common in men of Italian and other Southern European decent than in the Irish and other Northern European groups. The only mental illness that increased the risk of alcoholism was sociopathy.

3. *Biology has a larger impact than environment.* Early studies had suggested that childhood environment might predict alcoholism. The Core City sample at first appeared to confirm the hypothesis that warm and cohesive environments and close relationships were most characteristic of the men who did not become alcoholics. But further analysis showed that these differences generally could be accounted for by the presence or absence of an alcoholic biological parent. If alcoholism in biological parents is controlled, a troubled childhood environment does not appear to affect an individual's risk for alcoholism.

4. *Alcoholism appears to be progressive, but there is great variety in the patterns of this progression.* Some participants in this study developed alcoholism after a few months of abusive drinking. Others drank heavily for years before becoming alcoholics. For other participants, the disease remained chronic but relatively stable for years without getting better or worse.

5. *AA appears to be at least as effective as clinical treatment in helping alcoholics to begin stable abstinence.* Moreover, AA is much more important than clinical treatment in being able to help assure long-term stable recovery. Like treatment for other chronic diseases, ongoing treatment for alcoholism is necessary and AA provides daily or weekly help for years.

6. *Abstinence is necessary for long-term recovery.* There has always been a debate among researchers as to whether or not efforts in treatment to promote moderate or controlled drinking for alcoholics are either appropriate or possible.

AA and many medical and mental health professionals favor abstinence as the only solution; they believe that loss of control is inevitable once an alcoholic starts to drink. Advocates of controlled drinking often see alcohol dependence as a habit that can be modified by changing the circumstances that maintain it. They do not view it as a disease that needs treatment. Interestingly, Dr. Vaillant's study found out why this debate has been so clouded.

Vaillant's results showed that a short-term return to controlled drinking is possible for many alcoholics, but that a long-term return to controlled drinking is a rare and an unstable outcome. Though a return to controlled drinking for some alcoholics in the early stages of alcohol abuse is possible with the aid of therapeutic techniques, stable outcomes for these alcoholics are short lived. In the long haul, both the Core City and College samples demonstrate that abstinence is the most effective and stable treatment goal.

CHAPTER FIVE

Joe's Brain

What Happens in the Brain Chemistry
and Behavior of the Active Alcoholic

CURRENT TECHNOLOGY allows scientists to closely observe the brain of an alcoholic, including monitoring the brain while the subject performs intellectual tasks and experiences emotions. This technology allows us to map the interactions among nerve cells in the brain that occur as addiction progresses.

Joe is a lawyer suffering from a brain disease called alcoholism. Joe comes home from work every day and pours himself a rum and Coke into a thirty-two-ounce cup, goes into his den, and closes the door. Because his wife complains about his drinking, Joe starts keeping a bottle of rum in the car so he can have couple of drinks before he gets home. Joe thinks his wife is a pain. He feels practicing law is no fun because clients are always complaining, and he thinks that a couple of partners at the firm are becoming increasingly irritating. From Joe's perspective, life would be fine if the people around him did not cause so many problems.

What does Joe's brain look like? First, we know that Joe's brain is smaller and lighter than the brain of a nonalcoholic of the same age and gender because long-term alcohol use has caused Joe's brain to shrink. We are able to observe damage to Joe's brain even when there are not other clinical indicators of severe alcoholism (such as chronic liver disease or alcohol-induced dementia).

The shrinkage in Joe's brain is more extensive in the folded outer layer of the frontal lobe (cortex), which is understood to be the part of the brain that governs higher intellectual function. The rate of shrinkage in the area of Joe's brain responsible for developing trial strategies and coming up with good legal advice correlates with the amount of alcohol that he consumes. But not only is the "thinking" part of Joe's brain shrinking, other brain structures associated with memory as well as those associated with coordination and balance are shrinking also.

At home, when Joe drops into his easy chair, blood flow in his brain decreases and there is a reduction in the amount of communication between adjacent neurons. There is a decrease of blood flow in the area of Joe's brain where the neurotransmitter dopamine is present.

When Joe's wife comes into the den, interrupting his reverie to ask him about a bill collector's call, Joe reacts with rage that seems to come out of nowhere. When he yells at his wife, the frontal region of his brain reflects decreased metabolic activity, as compared with the brain of a nonalcoholic. This suggests a diminished capacity for dampening excessive neuronal activity and a weakening of Joe's ability to inhibit behavior.

The behaviors and feelings that alcoholism produces are well known. Tracking how these actually work in the brain will probably continue to confirm what scientific studies have shown to date—that one of the best treatments for alcoholism is based upon the Twelve Steps of AA. This research is already validating the experience that people find in recovery, where newfound sobriety is often described as being on a pink cloud. That pink cloud may be an apt metaphor to describe what happens when abstinence from alcohol allows more red blood to enter specific areas of the brain.

The good news for Joe is that recovery based on abstinence offers lots of hope. Cognitive function and motor coordination may improve at least partially within three to four weeks of abstinence, accompanied by at least partial reversal of brain shrinkage and some recovery of metabolic functions in the frontal lobes and cerebellum. Frontal lobe blood flow continues to increase with abstinence, returning to approximately normal levels within four years. As might be suspected, relapse to drinking leads to resumption of shrinkage, continued decline in metabolism and cognitive function, and damage to brain cells.

In the future, research may show why the organ most damaged by the disease of alcoholism—the brain—is also the organ that is most likely *not* to help the person suffering from the disease. The addicted lawyer will rationalize, minimize, and find a hundred good reasons why his or her problems stem from causes other than alcohol. The sick brain is not able to think itself into perceiving how the illness is affecting its owner's life.

Dr. William Silkworth, a pioneer in studying alcoholism, was one of the first physicians to state what would thereafter seem obvious—that alcoholism is a disease twofold in nature, being both a physical allergy and a mental obsession. As the craving, the physical allergy for alcohol—be it a pattern of daily evening drinking, weekend binges, or episodic drunkenness—becomes more and more ingrained, the mental obsession or delusion drives the person to believe that, despite the often severe consequences of the last drinking episode, no harm will be done by the next drink. Dr. Silkworth understood that the two primary protectors of health—reason and will—are of no use against this disease.

Increasingly, good treatment programs for addiction are available, but the prevailing public view about the disease of addiction limits their effectiveness. Many people believe that drug dependence is primarily a social problem that requires interdiction and law enforcement rather than a disease that requires prevention and treatment. The difficulty with this perception is that it lumps together the social problems associated with alcoholism and the medical problems of alcoholism—two vastly different areas—into a single analysis.

The social problems include those things that lead up to the possibility of alcoholism and other drug dependence. The medical problems include things that ensue once the onset of the disease of chemical dependence has occurred. Most of us don't mind helping those who have diseases, but we don't want to coddle social problems. Ironically, it is the social part of the problem—the part over which we have some control—that we, as a culture, are least interested in healing.

Joe grew up in a culture that encouraged drinking in college and in law school. For the most part, alcohol, marijuana, and other recreational drugs were an available part of the social scene. Media messages encourage us to believe that we have a right to instantaneous relief for any emotional discomfort. Alcohol is promoted as a way to achieve happiness. The truth is that we often coddle the social problem, which can create the opportunity for addictive disease to occur. Then, when the disease does attack a person, we may not utilize appropriate medical treatment. This occurs because alcoholism and other chemical dependencies are not like an acute infection where an antibiotic can be given and the patient can immediately get well. Rather, alcoholism and other chemical addictions are long-term chronic conditions that require ongoing attention.

In the October 4, 2000, issue of the *Journal of the American Medical Association*, drug dependence was compared with three other chronic illnesses: type 2 diabetes mellitus, hypertension, and asthma.[1] The authors of the article noted the many similarities among these chronic conditions and concluded that alcoholism and other drug addictions should be insured, treated, and evaluated just like other chronic illnesses.

Alcoholism requires medical treatment because it is a brain disease. Research has shown that addiction is not a matter of an individual's strength, moral character, willpower, or weakness. Instead, addiction can be attributed to the way an addicted person's brain is "wired" and altered by chronic use of alcohol and chemicals. For example, when non-addicts engage in healthy activities, such as taking a brisk walk, hugging a child, or holding the hand of a loved one, their brains release dopamine, a neuotransmitter naturally produced in the brain. Dopamine is produced to reward us, make us feel good, and offer a natural high. If the body gets large amounts of these feel-good chemicals from alcohol or other drugs on a regular basis, the brain will shut down its own factories that generate helpful, internal, natural "narcotics," such as dopamine. So after a while, because the individual's body is not producing its own dopamine, it needs to use more alcohol or other drugs just to feel normal again. Soon, he or she is hooked.

It is thought that addicted people have an overabundance of these natural neurotransmitters that result in emotional highs and lows, cravings, and feeling-driven behaviors. When a person who has this abnormal genetic pattern drinks alcohol, his or her brain creates a tremendous sense of satisfaction, relief, and pleasure. In the person with a predisposition toward addiction, the ingestion of alcohol or other drugs creates an intense euphoria that actually becomes its own reward.

For most of us, hugging a relative, reading a good book, seeing a great movie, or performing an enjoyable group activity stimulates the neurological reward that makes us feel good and gives our lives day-today meaning. For a significant percentage of the population that is bio-logically predisposed to addiction, drinking alcohol or using other drugs becomes a self-sustaining reward. For these individuals, a vicious cycle is established that drives them to drink more, creating more reward, which drives them to drink more, creating more reward, which drives them to drink more, and on and on. Without proper addiction treatment, this cycle can continue indefinitely.

CHAPTER SIX

Self-Deceptive Thinking

*Why Alcoholics Have Difficulty Admitting
They Have a Problem*

MANY ALCOHOLICS and other drug addicts deny that they have a problem. To the addicted and non-addicted person alike, this denial is one of the most frustrating and least understood aspects of the disease. Alcoholics and other drug addicts may lie to friends, family members, and physicians to try to conceal the amount or frequency of their substance use. Lying about use is one of the primary indications of addiction. In making a diagnosis of alcohol or other drug addiction, a good clinician will pay particular attention to the psychological manifestations of the disease. Does the individual lie about the amount he or she drinks or uses per day, per week, or per month? Does the person attempt to conceal the fact that he or she drinks alcohol or uses other drugs despite negative consequences, such as lack of nutrition, lack of sleep, failed relationships, or blackouts?

Some people think that denial is a form of mental illness. Non-addicted people suggest this because it seems "crazy" for the alcoholic to deny that he or she has a problem when his or her drinking is causing the destruction of finances, family, and career. The word "denial" implies that there is a conscious process of refusing to admit the problem, but a more accurate term to describe this phenomenon is "self-deception." Let's look at what happens.

An alcoholic has a biochemical compulsion to drink. If an individual drinks compulsively, he or she often gets drunk and eventually incurs negative consequences because of drinking. This is the basic progression of alcoholism. Two incompatible behaviors are created: first, the physiological need to drink, and second, the irresponsible behaviors that come with the altered mental and emotional state of intoxication. Self-deception is the process by which the psyche seeks to reconcile these two conflicting outcomes: (a) the physical need to drink, and (b) the negative physical behaviors that come with intoxication.

The brain tells the body, "I have to have this chemical." When the drug is ingested, the user engages in conduct that often violates his or her personal values. These two conflicting internal messages create a pressing need in the psyche for reconciliation, to bring about an inter-psychic truce so that the person can drink and not have severe mental anguish.

So how does the alcoholic accomplish this? He or she reconciles the conflict by developing a pattern of rationalizations, of self-deception that go something like this: "I don't mind being a little irresponsible. I have spent too much of my life being uptight." Or "I don't mind if my children don't have a sober father at home. They need a few challenges so they will be able to face the real world." Or "I don't mind drinking up the money I would use to send my kids to college because they will be a lot better off if they have to work for an education." In other words, there is a slow erosion of the individual's ordinary value system so that he or she never has to look at his or her alcohol use in a negative way. The trouble created by alcohol or other drug use isn't seen as trouble by the user. It is seen as problems created by others. Lawyers are particularly good at this self-deceptive thinking because they are trained to believe that every situation has two sides.

Denial is a way the alcoholic can justify drinking over and over again in spite of the resulting self-destructive problems. Denial is a defense mechanism that allows the neurobiological compulsion to be released. This same defense mechanism is seen with other diseases as well. Dr. Al Mooney, coauthor of *The Recovery Book* and medical director of the Durham Center in Durham, North Carolina, recalls, "I had a patient who was diagnosed with cancer. We talked about the problem and had a biopsy done. In our conversation she said, 'I know that you are fresh out of medical school, and you wouldn't know how to read one of those biopsies. I've been working in my kitchen all week and sweeping with my broom, which has left me with back pain. And I've had a cold lately, which caused the spot you see on my lungs.'" This patient's denial system took every piece of information used to confirm her diagnosis and explained it away to deny the fact that she had cancer.

This is the same thing that an alcoholic does, but in the case of the alcoholic, there is not just fear of a fatal disease that drives the self-deception, there is also a physical compulsion to drink. This is why it is so hard for people to understand the chemically addicted person, because his or her behavior often looks crazy or antisocial.

Why do active alcoholics and other drug addicts routinely lie to conceal their addiction? The reality is that most people do not want to be alone with their own feelings, with the reality of who they are. It is just not much fun. Lying is a way to avoid knowing one's self. Lying, as a behavior, is not something limited to alcoholics, but for alcoholics it is a psychological aspect that allows addiction to develop and flourish.

Lying is often a disease mode of the personality. Like a fever, it is part of an illness that initially occurs as a matter of the psyche's defense. Anytime the psyche is faced with overwhelming pressure, its defense is to compartmentalize or split. The ultimate pathological extreme of this is what is called a split personality, where two apparently entirely different personalities occupy one body. But in a normal personality, splitting is a way to deflect overwhelming grief, horror, or trauma. For example, the abused child sees the abuse as happening to someone else. After a psychologically injuring event has occurred, splits in the personality that were natural defenses must themselves be healed for good psychological development and maturity to occur.

Alcoholism destroys self-esteem. The psychological defense to this loss is either of two extremes—grandiosity or self-pity. An alcoholic may display both of these, but often grandiosity will be the defense of choice. The lack of self-esteem leads to a narcissistic, overinflated view of self. Lying is a way to perpetuate this form of self-centeredness. Getting off the merry-go-round of self-deception is often the hardest part of the addict's journey to get well.

In Dr. Charles Ford's book, *Lies! Lies!! Lies!!! The Psychology of Deceit*, the author examines a number of reasons for lying, including:[1]

- to avoid punishment
- to preserve a sense of autonomy
- as an act of aggression

- to obtain a sense of power
- as wish fulfillment
- as self-deception
- to manipulate the behavior of others
- to accommodate other self-deception
- to maintain self-esteem

Dr. Ford states, "We lie to ourselves and to others in an effort to support our sense of self-esteem, power, and individuality. We encourage other people to lie to us in order to support our own self-deceit." Lies are ways to avoid an awareness and acceptance of who we really are. Lies support self-esteem in a hollow way that ultimately undermines the support that is needed.

CHAPTER SEVEN

Addiction and Anger

How Addiction and Anger Interrelate

A FEW YEARS AGO I spoke at a continuing legal education program about lawyers and chemical addiction. I talked about the need to understand the signals we get from the dashboard of the physical/mental/emotional vehicle that we call the self.

After the program, I talked with a lawyer who told me that the only emotion he was aware of regularly experiencing was anger. It is my experience that anger and its aggressive expression can serve a lawyer in either a functional or dysfunctional way. Lawyers can use anger in a functional way as a source of energy to help a client repair an injustice. But some lawyers seem to run on anger all the time in order to get things done in their daily lives. Over time, the constant aggressiveness takes a toll. Anger may become difficult to turn off and can become a way of living, rather than just an emotion. Some may even say that being a lawyer is the profession of choice for individuals who thrive directly on anger, and for those who have the opposite problem—being afraid to deal with their own anger.

If a lawyer has repressed his or her anger and is out of touch with what causes this and other challenging emotions, then it is easy for that repressed anger to be redirected externally toward someone else. This is a way that some lawyers attempt to escape uncomfortable feelings.

For some individuals, alcohol offers a way to release anger and aggression. How many times have you seen a person attend a football game, drink a few beers, get mad at the referee, and act in an outrageous manner? It seems that our culture accepts alcohol consumption as an excuse for venting emotions that would otherwise not be appropriate.

For other individuals, alcohol may allow them to feel released from their unresolved anger. Still others may drink to drown their woes and forget their anger for a while.

There seems to be a common misconception that venting anger in an outwardly aggressive manner is a proper way to release the emotion. This is incorrect. In fact, the venting of anger may simply aggravate the situation and reinforce an unhealthy pattern of dealing with emotions without exploring their source or cause. This is where anger can seem to become an individual's whole being.

The emotion of anger is neither bad nor good. It is simply a signal of how an individual is experiencing the world. If an individual becomes mad over little things, it is often a clear sign that another emotional issue has been displaced and is trying to get attention. The challenge in dealing with anger is to understand what the signal means. Although the initial feeling of anger may seem automatic, an individual's response to the feeling is a matter of choice. Many people, including lawyers, fall into a conditioned response of avoidance or acting out without understanding what the self is trying to reveal about its experience of others and what is happening outside of the self.

Unresolved anger, or resentment, is counterproductive. Holding a grudge against another person does not affect that person; it only hurts the person holding the grudge. The physical consequences of ongoing resentment can include high blood pressure, headaches, and ulcers. It has been said that harboring resentments is like allowing someone whom you don't like to live rent-free inside your head. The use of alcohol or other drugs can be a way to nurse the grudge and provide ease from the discomfort the repressed anger has caused.

Unresolved anger is also a fundamental way that an individual may isolate himself or herself. Alcohol, or other drugs, may seem to offer a way to feel good inside this isolation. In fact, as substance abuse progresses, an addict often tends to drink or use more and more with increased isolation.

As lawyers, we must learn how to pay attention to our emotional messages and not act without thought. It is essential for us to seek to understand how we are feeling and not let emotions automatically run our lives.

If a lawyer doesn't recognize what the "dashboard light" of anger means when it is flashing, or if it seems to flash all the time, then he or she should talk with a professional counselor. If this lawyer uses substances to cope with the flashing light, then his or her best bet is to talk with a licensed therapist or counselor who can help.

CHAPTER EIGHT

The Walls We Build

The Four Major Changes in Personality Influenced by Addiction

MANY OF US with experience treating substance abuse are familiar with the negative behaviors that accompany alcoholism or other drug addictions. These behaviors include increased social and emotional isolation, failure to follow through where commitments have been made, and emotional manipulation of others. Along with these negative behaviors come changes in the addict's personality that result from the disease-driven necessity to put alcohol or other drugs ahead of other people, values, commitments, and deadlines—in other words, in front of everything else in life.

The personality changes that often accompany addiction are not unique; they are similar to changes that depression or life stresses may bring, which tend to isolate the individual. Usually, however, the addict's experience of these changes is a more extreme version of what some people may experience as normal parts of their personality.

The one certainty about life is that it is always changing. In daily life, these changes are sometimes dreaded—when we have to deal with death, illness, or job loss, for example. But change also brings growth. As new people come into our lives, we deepen our relationships with others and evolve and explore new interests. The active alcoholic often views change negatively because with an untreated chronic disease such as addiction, change means that he or she is getting worse. The reaction of the addicted psyche to change is to try to control people, places, and things—to build a wall around the psyche—so that the he or she will be insulated from change.

In my experiences with alcoholics and other addicts, there are four walls that addicted people build around their psyche. The first wall is guilt, which is often extremely harmful to others. A guilty lawyer will often neglect his or her spouse and children and target parents and siblings with unresolved anger. The guilty lawyer will inevitably begin to fail at work and let his or her law partners down. The result is that the addict is ridden with even more remorse and guilt. This guilt is so pervasive that it obscures how the addict actually feels. Guilt and remorse perpetuate the need to consume alcohol or other drugs to relieve the burden of this shame.

Holding on to guilt is often a system for living life based on the past. The addict is uncomfortable with feelings of guilt and will repress them, disregard them, blame someone else for them, and, in time, create more layers of guilt. The wall of guilt takes away freedom. When an individual lives with guilt, even good-intentioned acts seem to originate out of fear. For example, an alcoholic lawyer named Sarah may take a weekend trip to visit her parents. This act is not driven by what Sarah honestly wants to do, but instead is fueled by what she thinks she should do. This guilt-driven conduct is driven by past experiences and not the present reality. Sarah does not really know if she would like to go visit her parents because her guilt masks how she truly feels. In this pattern, life is driven by a pattern of regret from the past, which makes it almost impossible to be emotionally authentic. This sense of internal separation from the authentic self keeps others from being comfortable and further reinforces the addicted lawyer's isolation. This lawyer will often consume alcohol, or other drugs, in an effort to feel comfortable in his or her own skin.

The antidote to guilt is action. If a person determines that he or she did something shameful, then the solution is to promptly make amends for it. By making amends for our mistakes, we learn not to take that action again. We don't live in the past. This allows us to act honestly out of who we are in the present and experience life rather than observing ourselves in life.

The second wall around the addicted psyche is isolation. Lawyers must be able to judge, to determine the difference between right and wrong in every situation. While the ability to "ferret" out truth and separate right from wrong is essential to a lawyer's career, when it is a constant way of living, it is deadly. Being constantly critical of others is a way both to isolate and to avoid looking at our faults.

What addicts do not want to confront about themselves, they often project onto others. In order to avoid self-judgment, they erect a wall of judgment around the lives, values, and attitudes of everyone else. The more critical and judgmental the addict, the less other people enjoy being around him or her, which reinforces the addict's isolation.

The antidote to judgment is for a person to withdraw outward projections and take a look at his or her shortcomings. This is impossible in active addiction. In recovery, giving up judgments about others is a basic step to regaining a whole new sense of freedom and compassion. Addicts in recovery learn that they can enjoy the company of others, even though they don't agree with them about everything. This releases the huge burden of having to analyze the lives of others and allows the person in recovery to focus on the one person he or she *can* affect—himself or herself.

The third wall around the addicted psyche is self-centeredness. Addiction focuses an individual's thoughts, actions, and emotions around the substance of use. The addict is consumed with asking questions: "Where will I get the next drink/fix?" "When will I be able to get it?" "Will I be able to get enough?" This pattern of self-centeredness arises from the need to obtain the drug of choice, but after a while it can become a way of living that pervades the addict's personality. Self-centeredness, or narcissism, can manifest as attention seeking, grandiosity, vanity, arrogance, false modesty, and self-pity. The addict may sway between passive and aggressive extremes. For example, the addict's pride may drive him or her to try to get attention aggressively then, a moment later, he or she will try to get attention passively. Often the addict will exhibit both passiveness and aggressiveness in different circumstances. Both seek meaning for this individual's life through vanity—trying to control what others think.

Active addiction, because it undermines all internal emotional security, quickly leads to excessive attempts to satisfy natural instincts for security, acceptance, and sex. Excessive pride may not be the breeder of human difficulties as much as it is a false rationalization created to justify the excesses of the individual's natural drives. However this self-centeredness is manifest, either in grandiosity or victimization, it is not pleasant for others to be around. These destructive ways of being can drive healthy people away, again reinforcing the isolation of the addict.

The fourth wall is the development of an "all or nothing" view of life. All four walls take away freedom, but this wall takes away more than the others. As the addict's disease progresses, he or she begins to see all choices in black and white. The addict thinks, "I must stay with my nagging husband or leave him" or "I must continue with my sixty-hour-a-week job or become unemployed." The addicted mind begins to be unable to conceive of the possibility that changes might occur in the marriage or career that are beneficial.

This attitude can stem from the addict's propensity for extremes—in telling himself or herself, "I either drink or I don't drink." For the addict, neither of these options is acceptable, but they can seem to be the only ones available. There is no way for alcoholics to drink and not have chaos, and there is no way for them to imagine that they can abstain and still have a happy and meaningful life. The "all or nothing" nature of addiction colors how the alcoholic sees the rest of his or her life. The possibility of trying something new—the possibility of failing—is viewed as too scary, much like the unknown world of recovery. The "all or nothing" wall is very isolating because there is no creativity, no opportunity to try something new or to try and fail. This wall represents the loss of hope.

Active addicts seem to need these four walls. They help to create the illusion that change can be controlled, that the inevitable course of the disease will not affect them. In recovery, an individual can experience the freedom to take an objective look to see if he or she built these walls in order to survive a painful life experience. It is possible to experience more freedom and joy in life by taking these walls down. For the lawyer in active addiction, it is virtually impossible to demolish these walls without help. Demolishing walls does require some "heavy lifting," and the task is best accomplished with the help of a professional counselor, addiction treatment professional, and a recovery support group.

CHAPTER NINE

AA and the Establishment Clause

The Most Successful Treatment for Addiction
Is Not a Religion

ALCOHOLISM AND OTHER DRUG ADDICTIONS, like many chronic long-term diseases, require ongoing attention to ensure that once the disease is in remission, it stays there. In my experience, the most effective method to keep alcoholism in remission is participation in Alcoholics Anonymous (AA). Because of this, many prison, probation, or other state-related programs have referred or required addicted persons to participate in AA. The underlying premise of AA is that alcoholism is a disease that affects an individual physically (remedied through abstinence), emotionally (through group support and sponsorship), and spiritually (through establishing a relationship with a Higher Power).

In "Religion and Rehabilitation: The Requisition of God by the State," Derek P. Apanovitch reviews cases that have dealt with AA and the Establishment Clause.[1] All of these cases, without discussion, assume a deconstructed, rationalist view of humans—that we are physical and emotional creatures but have no inherent spiritual nature. Because of this reductionist view, the courts equate the spiritual component in AA with religion, even though, both in fact and theory, AA does not promote religion.

Religion has traditionally been the path for human's spiritual nature to be developed. Our courts have confused a map of spiritual beliefs, often inherent in religious practices, with a direct experience of human spiritual nature. Secular thinking has led to a denial of our spiritual nature and equated the various forms of responses to that nature (different religions) with the nature itself. AA provides an opportunity to experience each individual's spiritual nature, not to promote set beliefs about what that nature should look or be like.

What primarily separates spirituality from religion is that spirituality is encountered as experience, while religion has more to do with sets of beliefs. And while different religious beliefs may be seen as ways to enter into a path of spiritual experience, the founders of AA, through their own experiences, found that an individual's spiritual nature and the opportunity for spiritual experience exist apart from any particular set of religious beliefs.

Asking a prisoner to explore his or her spiritual nature by going to AA is analogous to requiring him or her to go to the exercise grounds or to see a therapist. The prisoner may not willingly participate but at least will have the opportunity to improve his or her physical and emotional well-being. We don't question the state's right to seek to rehabilitate prisoners. We don't limit the prison's authority to send only those inmates to exercise who believe exercise is good for them. Nor do we assume that by requiring exposure to exercise that the state is requiring the prisoner to believe in basketball but not in jogging. We don't require any particular belief; we just require the opportunity for an experience of positive physical activity.

Alcoholics Anonymous does not require that a participant believe in any organized religion or pray to an iconic God such as Christ or Buddha. Instead, AA offers the opportunity for an individual's spiritual nature to be addressed through his or her own individual definition of spirituality. AA doesn't ask a person to forgive in the name of any certain religion, but it teaches through experience the power of forgiveness. AA doesn't require an individual to meditate in Buddhist or Hindu fashion, but it does show that the experience of meditation can have positive affects on human nature in a spiritual way. The prisoner can show up for the basketball game and yet not play; he or she can go to AA meetings and not listen or share. There is no way to force engagement, but it is possible to require exposure to something that may be helpful.

Establishment Clause case law is, in part, overly cumbersome and complex, because it defines human nature with reductionism. Perhaps part of this confusion stems from the fact that religion itself has often been confused about humans' spiritual nature and sought to impose its own set of views as part of its definition of that nature. What AA has given alcoholics is a true example of a structure that can attempt to nurture their spiritual nature without imposing a religious viewpoint. The alcoholics are left then with the challenge to work, not just on the exterior level, but also on the interior level.

Most Lawyer Assistance Programs (LAPs) across the country facilitate Twelve Step support groups for lawyers suffering from addiction, depression, or both. Participation in these groups is always voluntary, so no Establishment Clause issues arise. The LAPs promote group support for the same reason they may promote pharmacological and counseling treatment of depression. For a properly diagnosed patient, these treatments may work, and together may offer maximum help. In fact, each treatment method addresses an aspect of our human nature—physical, emotional, and spiritual. Group support can help addicted or depressed lawyers, just as group support helps cancer patients.

Our spiritual nature exists, however we choose to label it. Spirituality can be experienced in a negative way that leads to isolation and self-destruction. Or it can be positive and life-giving. I expect that it is difficult for non-addicted intellectuals, who see humans as non-spiritual beings limited by ego, to imagine what it is like for a depressed, atheist lawyer to find that a Twelve Step program of recovery offers a way back to his or her spiritual nature that makes life blossom with new hope and vitality. I can report to you that I don't need to imagine it. I have seen it work. For each person who makes this discovery, the experience is unique, though universal, and profoundly healing.

CHAPTER TEN

Redefining God

Why the Twelve Steps Work

FOR THOSE OF US who grew up in the twentieth century, we are indeed fortunate that there evolved, out of the efforts of the founders of AA, a modern shorthand method of dethroning the bruised, addicted ego and all its baggage. This method is called the Twelve Steps. The Twelve Steps give addicted people, no matter how broken they may feel, hope that they can feel the gift of membership in the human race.

The founders of AA discovered that the key to the healing process was to admit powerlessness against the disease of addiction. This requires that an addicted individual surrender not only to the disease, but surrender the ego's battle to control the disease. Once this occurs there is space in the psyche for something new to come take the place of the false meaning supplied by using alcohol or other drugs. The founders of AA realized that this "new thing" must be spiritual in nature, because if it were emotional, a new craving would be set up. Fitting our individualistic society, the founders of AA also understood that this new spiritual source of connection must be different for each individual, and so they termed this source "Higher Power."

The subtle genius of AA's development of the Twelve Steps and the concept of a Higher Power was allowing each individual to define what this "Power" might be. Often this Power ends up in the form of a traditional religious idea that the individual may have thought he or she had rejected long ago. But many times the Higher Power is something that has no religious connection whatsoever.

Regardless of how an individual defines his or her Higher Power, what is indeed dramatic is the psychic shift that occurs as the ego-based "gods" of manipulation and control drop away. What happens is something like this: After accepting the guidance of a Higher Power, there is no longer the ego separation between what an individual *wants* to do and what the individual thinks he or she *ought* to do; there is just doing what the Higher Power says is the "next right thing." Life becomes not about obligation but instead about opportunity. Life is not about "shoulds" or "should nots" but instead is about freedom and choice. Life is not about wanting to avoid the results of our actions but about being happily and responsibly committed to each action.

With a Higher Power as a guide, life becomes more relaxed and it flows; it is no longer about teeth-gritting willpower. There is a sense of inner peace even in troubled times, as opposed to only feeling peaceful when things are going as expected. There is an inner sense of rightness, while self-doubt and second-guessing melt away. There is a healthy detachment from opinions of others as opposed to a need for assurance and approval. Energy seems to return promptly upon rest after a hard task; rather than seeming a scarce commodity in an exhausting uphill process. There is a sense of purpose to life and the feeling of "rightness" comes as a quiet and inner knowing, as opposed to the ego's momentary rush of excitement. As the lesser gods of manipulation and control fade away, life seems to have all kinds of wonderful serendipity.

This Higher Power can be described in many ways, but it is a relation with an individual's inner self and the meaning he or she creates outside of the self. This relationship becomes the individual's reason for living—it makes a place for him or her to be human in this world. Once this new spiritual connection with the Higher Power occurs— once there is a grounded sense of self that is not pulled at by the whim of cravings in order to feel okay—then the addicted person is ready to have interpersonal relations from a position of inner stability and to give meaning to what it is like to be human.

CHAPTER ELEVEN

Codependency and Addiction

The Lingering Impact on Children of Addicted Parents

WHEN A CHILD lives in a family where addiction or mental illness exists, he or she may grow up denying emotional reality in order to survive. Maybe that emotional reality is alcoholism, rage, abandonment, incest, parental fighting, or coping with a workaholic parent. It doesn't matter; the end results are similar.

In these families, the messages parents send their children include "Children should be seen, not heard," "Big boys don't cry," and "Girls don't get angry." In other words, these children grow up in the middle of a war with their emotional selves. To survive, they often have to discount and ignore their feelings. They do this because there is no safe place to learn who they are emotionally. The survival mechanism often works. These children survive, but the cost is that they never learn who they are as emotional beings.

When there is no safe place for a child to learn to experience and discover who he or she is, this child's feelings of identity can become (and remain throughout adulthood) hinged on externals: what others think, approval of peers or bosses, recognition at work, popularity, spousal approval, or even what his or her children do for work.

The trauma of feeling unsafe in childhood (particularly if this trauma is experienced daily for years and years) makes it very difficult to feel safe emotionally later in life, even with a string of accomplishments attached to his or her name. When these children become adults and are exposed to alcohol or other drugs in a social way, they may develop a pattern of drinking or using drugs, quite unobserved over time, that allows avoidance of these uncomfortable feelings of emptiness or uneasiness. Whether the individual is aware or unaware of medicating his or her feelings, the pattern of family addiction is apt to be repeated.

Author Sharon Wegscheider-Cruse has found that children who grow up with an addicted parent often develop one or a combination of the following survival skills, which they carry into adulthood.[1] These skills initially may help the young child cope but will hold the adult child back, in relationships, career, and life.

1. The Hero: This child tries to excel in order to prove his or her self-worth. The hero is often the mediator between the parents, one or both of whom are struggling with addiction, and tries to feel a sense of belonging by trying to "fix the family."
2. The Enabler: This child will do anything to avoid emotional pain. If necessary, he or she will even help provide alcohol or other drugs to the addicted parent, which will enable the cycle of drinking or using to continue.
3. The Scapegoat: This child becomes angry in response to the emotional uncertainty of living with an addicted parent. Often this child will, in all outward appearances, be functioning normally, but is actually breaking rules, causing trouble in the community, and having difficulties at school. The scapegoat helps keep the attention away from the alcoholic by creating more public problems, which become the focus of attention.
4. The Lost Child: This child's response to the emotional uncertainty of living with an addicted parent is to try to disappear. This child tries to blend in and not be noticed. This is the quiet child who spends excessive time in front of the computer or in fantasy games that keep the child safe from reality.
5. The Mascot: This child's response to the frustrated emotional needs of alcoholism is to get attention and validation by providing laughter. Humor is a primary survival skill. This child tries to divert the family's attention toward anything outside the ongoing family crisis.

Many counselors working in Lawyer Assistance Programs (LAPs) have experience advising adult children of alcoholics or other addicts.

These adult children have often strived for a lifetime to survive their parent's addiction, and they contact an LAP to get help. For example, a male lawyer recently told me he was burned out with the legal profession. He said that it was hard for him to come in to work and that he hated returning calls. His relationship with his spouse was poor, and his child was acting out in school by skipping classes and smoking marijuana.

There was an inner war raging inside this lawyer. Part of him was trying as best he could to get the approval of his clients and law firm. He wanted to feel at home in the legal profession. He wanted his career to be a safe place, but he grew up in a home with an alcoholic parent and he was still struggling to find a sense of security he never had as a child. He and the rest of the family had been consumed with trying to please the alcoholic father. The lawyer never had a meaningful emotional connection with his father and tried, in lieu of that, to win his father's approval by doing well in school. This lawyer succeeded in college and law school, but these external achievements never compensated for the lack of connection with his father.

After law school, this lawyer realized he was drinking heavily and immediately gave up alcohol because he didn't want to be like his father. The alcohol had done a good job of masking the underlying irritability and discontent the lawyer felt. Without alcohol, he tried to avoid these feelings by simply moving on to accomplish the next thing on his list of things a law career should have (or at least what he thought it should have) in order to feel okay. This illness is most accurately described as delayed stress syndrome but is more commonly termed codependency.

Codependency is a very vicious and powerful stress disorder. Like alcoholism or drug addiction, one of the most salient aspects of codependency is that the survival skill that was erected to soften the blow of the trauma effectively prevents the individual from seeing how sick he or she is.

This can't be said too loudly—if an individual is codependent, he or she may feel that he or she has a "dis-ease" with life, but often the person will not see the extent to which his or her emotional being has been warped and distorted by an underlying trauma in his or her childhood. This is because of the psychic numbing effect created to blunt the trauma. Like the stress reaction, the psychic response of deadened feelings that is experienced with trauma may last for years after the traumatic episode.

Codependency is a malediction in which an individual looks outside himself or herself to other people, places, and things—to money and prestige—to determine if he or she has worth. Because these external conditions can change, the individual is inherently insecure, which leaves the codependent person often feeling like a victim. Codependent lawyers often don't see themselves as victims. This is because lawyers are the ones who are supposed to help victims of injustice. Instead, codependent lawyers may feel depressed and frustrated; they may feel that their spouses, partners, and clients don't understand how hard legal work is and what the work is like.

Since lawyers don't like to identify themselves as victims, they may compensate by victimizing other people in order to feel okay. They may use this energy to run their work life. We have come to understand more completely the forms of personality reaction to unperceived trauma. The following four personality adaptations can often be found in codependent individuals:

1. The Uncaring Aggressive: This is the hard-driving person who cannot tolerate any type of human weakness in others, because to do so would require him or her to accept his or her own weakness and vulnerability. This is the "steamroller" lawyer who invariably applies a sledgehammer to a small tack when a light hammer would suffice.

2. The Self-Righteous Aggressive: This lawyer thinks that he or she always knows what is right for others and what other people should do. This lawyer feels the great burden of having to do it all because other people do not know the right way to do things.

3. The Passive Aggressive: This lawyer acts friendly to others but sabotages them in any way possible. This lawyer sees himself or herself as a wonderful person who is treated unfairly by "the system." This lawyer feels like a victim and feels so vulnerable that he or she cannot face conflict directly.

4. The Martyr: This is the individual who is classically seen as

codependent. Martyr lawyers use guilt as a way to try to manipulate others.

These are broad categories and may overlap. An individual may use different styles of defense in different situations. These defenses are all guises to protect the individual from feeling emotions that were long ago suppressed by trauma. Codependent people often don't feel equal to others—everyone else is either above them, to whom they are overly deferential, or below them, to whom they are abusive and condescending.

Codependency is a dysfunctional relation with one's own body, mind, emotions, and spirit. When an individual has a dysfunctional relationship with himself or herself, it can cause dysfunctional relationships with others. Codependent individuals will often try to fill the hole inside themselves with a relationship, a series of relationships, booze, or work—but none of these succeed. Recovery must start with dismantling the self-limiting view of experience. This is a difficult process for lawyers because they find security in thinking they know all or most of the answers. But for the emotional numbness to thaw, they have to start with the recognition that their understanding is limited—that the way each of us operates in the world as a reflection of our life experience is inadequate and imperfect.

Once there is a willingness to accept the idea that the codependent individual's system for knowing emotional truth is broken, then he or she can begin to bring into consciousness those beliefs and attitudes from his or her own subconscious that are causing the dysfunctional reactions. Then the codependent person can begin to find a new emotional truth that allows for trust and love rather than have a life driven by rage, shame, and guilt. Ultimately, recovery from codependency is a wonderful process because it involves the grand journey of self-discovery—of finding out who we really are.

The good news is that more and more treatment centers are recognizing the family systems nature of addictive disease. Most treatment programs offer family weeks to help provide enough initial insight for family members to understand their need to get the kind of assistance necessary to deal with the affects of alcoholism on their lives. When the alcoholic, the spouse, and the child all get help, then the chances are great that the family can move forward in a positive and healthy way.

CHAPTER TWELVE

Stress

Understanding the Link between Stress and Health

MANY OF US UNDERSTAND that extreme emotional disturbances can adversely affect our health. This recognition that stress can make us sick is not new. Centuries ago doctors recognized that two individuals could get the same disease yet the courses of their illness could be quite different in ways that reflected the personal characteristics of the individuals. Today, science is beginning to understand why this is so, and we are beginning to understand the inquiries we can make about any disease state, such as: Why is stress seemingly something that causes high achievement in some and disease in others? How does stress interact with personality differences? Does stress cause depression? What does stress have to do with how fast we age and how well our memories work?

Like a gazelle being chased by a lion, the human body is brilliantly designed to deal with acute physical stress. In the stress response, energy is mobilized and delivered to large muscle tissues that need it to either flee or fight, long-term body repairs are put on hold, the immune system lets down, pain is blunted, and cognition is sharpened. We all understand the logic of the body's fight or flight response to acute physical stress. In addition, the body even does a pretty good job of dealing with chronic physical stressors such as being caught in a famine that lasts six months.

But most stress doesn't come from lions or famine. It arises inside the mind. Gazelles don't worry if their retirement income will last. But humans generate all sorts of stressful events purely from imagining or anticipating them.

The problem is, when an individual sits around worrying about stressful things, he or she is turning on the same physiological response as the gazelle being chased by the lion. Done repeatedly, this causes enormous problems for the physical system. Some lawyers get used to and like the rush stress brings, especially when it heightens mental acuity.

Initially, scientists thought that the problems caused by prolonged stress were due to the fact that hormones, secreted during stress, were depleted. Science has found that the problem is not so much that the stress hormones run out, but rather that these stress hormones cause the body damage. This makes sense because the stress response is designed to sacrifice everything for the short-term goal of surviving an immediate threat. If you repeatedly turn on the stress response, or if you cannot appropriately turn off the stress response at the end of a stressful event, the stress response itself can become as damaging as the triggering event. In other words, it is not that the unmanaged stress response *makes* you ill, it's that it increases your *risk* of illness.

Every now and then a news article reports a tremendously stressful accident or event. Of those persons who endured the event, some will talk about how difficult it was but will seem after a while to have gotten over it and be okay. Another group of persons will suffer from posttraumatic stress syndrome, need extensive psychological treatment, and may have difficulty functioning for the rest of their lives. Then there will be a few who will say the event was really horrible but that the experience allowed them to realize what was really important and precious in life. While these people wouldn't want to do it again, the experience was significant to them in a profound and meaningful way.

This extreme example of stress tells us something really important—the context in which stress-induced disease arises and the nature of each individual's psychological and physiological reaction to stress may dictate whether stress causes disease in an individual or, in fact, increases resiliency.

Let's move from an overview of the stress response to a closer examination of physiological effects of the stress response. What is happening to a lawyer physically as he or she gears up for a first trial, shows up at a trial unprepared, or is sent back to the office by the senior partner to get in those 1,800 billable hours? The internal activities of his or her body shift immediately, the digestive tract shuts down, and the breathing rate skyrockets. Secretion of sex hormones is inhibited, while the hormones epinephrine, norepinephrine, and glucocorticoid pour into the bloodstream.

Central to the stress response is the change in cardiovascular response. Blood begins moving faster and with more force. In the face of a maximum stressor, the heart's output increases over five times. To get more blood to your muscles for fight or flight, the sympathetic nervous system, in conjunction with glucocorticoid, constricts certain major arteries. As a result, blood is delivered with greater speed to certain muscles.

At the same time, there is a dramatic decrease in blood flow to uninvolved parts of the body, including the digestive tract, kidneys, and skin. To conserve body fluids, the brain sends an additional stress response to the kidneys, telling them to stop the process of eliminating waste and water. Water from the kidneys is reabsorbed into the body. Because water in the bladder cannot be reabsorbed, and its weight is an impediment to flight, the message is sent for the bladder to be emptied.

The impact of the stress response on the cardiovascular system is incremental. The body works harder for a while, and if it does so on a regular basis, the cardiovascular system wears out sooner. With the chronic increase in blood pressure that accompanies repeated stress, damage begins to occur at branch points in arteries throughout the body. The smooth inner lining of the blood vessels begins to tear, scar, and pit. Once this layer is damaged, the fatty acids and glucose that are mobilized in the bloodstream by the onset of the stress response begin to work their way under the vessel lining, causing it to thicken. This is how chronic stress causes arteriosclerosis.

Heart disease is the number one killer in the United States. Dramatic evidence of the connection between the stress response and heart disease is the number of times that a cardiac catastrophe occurs when the victim is under substantial stress. Remember Bill Hodgman, one of the prosecutors in the O. J. Simpson trial? He got chest pains and collapsed around the twentieth time he jumped up to object during Johnnie Cochran's witness examinations.

Let's turn from the cardiovascular system to how the body's energy-making system reacts to stress. Again, the significant point here is that the manner in which stress causes the body to mobilize energy can create conditions favorable to causing illness. The stress response halts the storage of energy and begins to liquidate energy already stored. The body does this through the release of the stress hormones glucocorticoid, epinephrine, and norepinephrine, which cause free fatty acids and glycerol to pour into the circulatory system. On the most basic level, this is inefficient. If an individual activates the stress response too often, he or she will expend so much energy that tiredness and fatigue are inevitable. With enough stress, diabetes can result.

As I have already mentioned, digestion is quickly shut down during the stress response. This occurs in the stomach and small intestine. The opposite occurs in the large intestine where the body's objective, as with the bladder, is to eliminate excess baggage as quickly as possible. The result is diarrhea. The connection between stress, colitis, and irritable bowel syndrome is more complex. Stress appears to worsen both conditions, but exactly how it does so is still unclear. These conditions may result in part from a diet lacking in fiber. While a lawyer's stress response may routinely eliminate waste from the colon, at the same time the digestive process is stalled in the stomach and small intestine, causing the entire digestive tract to be put under strain, much like pressing the brake and the accelerator at the same time.

One thing that is so disturbing about the stress response is its pervasive effect on almost all of the body's systems. Almost no physical system is exempt from the effects of the stress response, including sex and reproduction. With the onset of stress, the entire sexual hormone secretion system is inhibited. Erections become more difficult for men, and women may find their menstrual cycles become irregular.

One of the newer areas of stress research focuses on how stress affects memory. Memory is not monolithic. There are several different types of memory, most notably short-term, long-term, and remote memory. Just as there are different types of memory, different parts of the brain are involved in memory storage and retrieval. Memory is not stored in specific neurons, but in the patterns of excitation of vast arrays of neurons.

We know that initially stress heightens mental acuity as well as energy. More oxygen is delivered to the brain (as well as the muscles to be used in fight or flight). The difficulty is in the extended stress response. New evidence suggests that continued exposure to stress could compromise the ability of neurons to survive neurological disease.

The same research that suggests that the stress response can damage our memories also suggests that it may affect aging by accelerating aging of the brain. In addition, the older we get, the longer it takes our body to reestablish its normal equilibriums. As we get older we become less flexible, physiologically as well as psychologically. The cardiac muscle gets stiffer. Aged organisms not only have trouble turning off the stress response after the stressor is removed or has ended, but they also secrete more stress-related hormones even in their normal, non-stressed state.

Some lawyers are good at modulating the effects of stress and others are not. The repeated stress of complex trial work may make one person a great lawyer, while in another attorney it may create the conditions for illness. One of the hugely variable factors is personality. The level of stress we are under and the nature of our personalities affect the context in which disease arises at the cellular level. Those who handle stress well do so because of natural tendencies in their personality to exercise or use other outlets to decrease the effects of the stress response. Creating good habits, such as physical exercise and recreation, can help reduce the impact of stress on the body.

Social support is another proven way to reduce the impact of stress. Social support comes when we are in relation with other people—those with whom we can discuss exactly what is going on and be heard without judgment. This can occur in both structured and unstructured settings. Studies have also shown that individuals who are socially isolated have overly active sympathetic nervous systems. This leads to the likelihood of higher blood pressure and increased risk of heart disease to go with the risk from the stress response.

A third factor is how we deal with unpredictability. Those who need greater predictability are less able to moderate the effects of the stress response. If our control needs are high over areas of our lives where we have little control, then the stress response will often remain stuck in the ON position. Twelve Step programs offer a way to moderate control needs, to adjust to the ultimate reality that everything always changes.

Conversely, the ability to have control over certain things, to have a passion in life, and to have a purpose are all important psychological factors in alleviating the stress response. Somehow the stressful things in life take less of a toll when there is a course set, especially a flexible one, for an individual's life direction.

The good news, then, is that there are psychological ways of living that we can have by natural predisposition, or that we can develop, that lessen the impact of the stress response. These include an inclination toward exercise, a tendency to avoid isolation, and a positive attitude toward the unpredictable nature of life. The bad news is that these internal psychological factors are so powerful that they can trigger a stress response on their own, or make another stressor much more stressful.

The first step toward increased health is to be aware of these stressors and how they affect us. Professionals seeking to help lawyers deal with stress might ask, "What are this individual lawyer's strengths and weaknesses for coping with common stressors?" Each individual lawyer needs to develop proactive strategies so that the effects of the stress response don't dominate his or her life.

CHAPTER THIRTEEN

Reducing Stress with Alcohol
The Connections between Stress and Alcohol Use

Speak no more of her. Give me a bowl of wine.
In this I bury all unkindness . . .
—William Shakespeare, *Julius Caesar*

WHILE SPEAKING TO GROUPS OF LAWYERS, I often ask the question, "Why do we drink?" The answer is always, "We drink because it works." What works is the relationship between alcohol and the emotional experience of stress. For hundreds of years, as the Shakespeare quote at the beginning of this chapter suggests, people have observed a relationship between alcohol consumption and stress. Our common cultural belief is that both social drinkers and problem drinkers can reduce stress by drinking. We see it in the movies all the time—to reduce stress, just pour yourself a strong drink.

Researchers believe that alcohol's anticipated stress-relieving effect is a primary motivation for many people's consumption of alcohol, despite the potentially harmful consequences of drinking. Our own experience and our cultural messages tell us the same thing—that drinking will alter our mood in a way that will make our mood less stressed and more pleasurable.

The question then is this: If this is what we believe happens, does it in fact happen? The answer is not as simple as we would like it to be. First, there is substantial evidence to support our personal experience and the cultural message that alcohol consumption *can* reduce the magnitude of an individual's response to stress. But research published by the National Institutes of Health (NIH) in 1999 has shown, to the surprise of many investigators, that the relationship between alcohol and stress reduction is inconsistent.

There are complex variables that condition the effect of alcohol on stress among lawyers. A key factor that applies to lawyers, and everyone else, is family history. We know that children of alcoholics are at heightened risk of becoming problem drinkers compared with children of nonalcoholics. Some research suggests that alcohol consumption may produce an enhanced stress-response dampening among individuals who are at greater risk for alcoholism. In other words, individuals who are more predisposed to alcoholism may, because of the way their brain handles alcohol, get a greater stress-dampening response than individuals who are less predisposed to alcoholism.

Although the research on those persons who have enhanced stress-response dampening from drinking is far from clear, it suggests that, if drinking seems to bring a certain lawyer greater stress reduction than it offers other lawyers under similar stress, this might be a clue that alcoholism could be a potential problem for that lawyer. After a lawyer becomes an alcoholic, the lawyer gradually loses the emotional lift from drinking, and is eventually drinking to try to feel normal again.

Another theory that affects lawyers particularly, and which has been the subject of research, is the idea that people who are highly self-conscious are most likely to experience alcohol's stress-response dampening and to get a subtle reinforcing message to drink because of the extent of that dampening. According to this theory, people who are self-aware often internally evaluate their own performance and may experience stress if the result of that self-evaluation is negative. Alcohol consumption impairs the drinker's ability to process information from the environment with respect to himself or herself. Thus the use of alcohol by the self-aware person has a stress-response dampening effect, whether or not there is stress coming from the outside environment. For lawyers who go around with a self-critical voice in their head, the use of alcohol may be the easiest and most effective way to quiet that voice. This stress reduction has a reinforcing effect, thereby increasing the probability of increased drinking.

Another factor affecting whether or not alcohol consumption reduces stress is where the drinking occurs. If a lawyer goes out after work and drinks with people who talk about sports and not about law practice, there is a greater likelihood he or she will experience positive stress reduction. If a lawyer goes home and drinks alone, a stress-dampening response from drinking is unlikely and stress may even increase because the drinker's attention may remain focused on the then salient stressor. Of course, if the lawyer has developed dependency on alcohol, then the repetitious drinking is going to occur whether or not it produces a reduction in the emotional experience of stress.

So what are the red flags that are raised by the relationship between alcohol use and stress dampening? First, if a lawyer is alcohol dependent, the ability of alcohol to reduce the stress has already begun to fade and will continue to fade over time. Second, if a lawyer is not alcohol dependent but feels that alcohol relieves the stress in him or her more than in "normal" drinkers, this lawyer may have a problem that results in alcoholism. Third, alcohol is perhaps at its best as a stress reducer when used as a part of other pleasurable activities, such as watching or talking about sports. If, however, the use of alcohol becomes the principal reason for engaging in certain activities or sports, then the use of alcohol has already become problematic. Fourth, if a lawyer usually drinks in isolation (or drinks with the same person and complains about the same problems), chances are that alcohol will not reduce his or her stress level, but will actually make it worse, which in turn becomes a good motivation to drink more. Fifth, if a lawyer generates some of his or her own stress internally—by engaging in perfectionist behaviors—then it is possible that he or she will be more likely to drink in a manner that reinforces the use of alcohol and leads to alcoholism.

CHAPTER FOURTEEN

Alcoholism in Older Adults

The Challenge in Preventing and Treating Adult Alcoholism

IT SEEMS THAT IN AMERICAN CULTURE we have a double-standard attitude about drinking among older adults. Alcohol consumption that would not be tolerated among young people is often tolerated or encouraged among older adults. This attitude is reflected in statements such as, "Well, old Joe is retired now and he deserves to get a little 'potted' every afternoon if he wants." Or "Sure, Mary is a little tipsy every day, but she is not hurting anyone." Perhaps both these older adults have slipped into alcoholism, a disease that destroys the quality of an individual's emotional, spiritual, and physical life. What if another disease were involved? Would we be so anxious to dismiss symptoms of tuberculosis and encourage the perpetuation of a disease afflicting a loved one, including neglecting to see that treatment is provided?

Seniors must consume alcohol with caution because as our bodies age, they metabolize alcohol more slowly. The *Dietary Guidelines for Americans 2005* report states that, "Those who drink alcoholic beverages should do so in moderation—up to one drink per day for women and up to two drinks per day for men."[1] One drink is defined as 5 ounces of wine, 12 ounces of regular beer, or 1.5 ounces of 80-proof distilled spirits. Many older adults have medical conditions that lead them to consume daily prescription medications, and many of these drugs are sedatives. In these cases, extreme care should be taken, because some prescription drugs interact with alcohol in a way that decreases the efficacy of the drug being taken and/or increases the effect of the alcohol being consumed.

Older adults often have to deal with loss. Many lawyers feel a loss of identity after retirement or after switching to a less-active law practice. This is also a time in life when many people have to deal with the loss of a spouse, family members, and friends. Many older adults who have lived highly successful lives in their earlier years, perhaps in a sense because of their earlier successes, are not emotionally experienced in how to deal with loss and do not know how to grow through the grief process. Those who haven't learned how to experience life losses in positive ways are very vulnerable to late-onset addiction.

Many physicians are not good at spotting addiction problems among older adults. The National Center on Addiction and Substance Abuse at Columbia University presented a hypothetical case of an older woman with alcoholism to a group of four hundred doctors. Almost all the doctors overlooked alcohol as a potential problem in their diagnosis.

The stereotype of what an alcoholic looks like in older age is that of the person who has been drinking excessively for years. It does not include the person whose addiction has commenced because of changes in work and lifestyle in his or her older years.

I have found that older lawyers, especially those who have successful careers, are likely to view addiction as more of a moral problem than a disease. For them it is hard to get help because of the shame they experience about having this kind of a problem. They end up suffering in isolation. Retirement can create social isolation. Addiction will only make this isolation worse. There is some good news. Many addiction treatment centers now offer specialized programs available for older adults seeking recovery.

CHAPTER FIFTEEN

Compulsive Gambling

Understanding the Nature of a Process Addiction

GAMBLING IS NOW LEGAL in many states. Because of this, it is logical that there has been an increase in problem gambling in the United States. Gambling is defined as any betting or wagering, for self or others, whether for money or not, no matter how slight or insignificant, where the outcome is uncertain or depends upon chance or skill. These games of chance include card games, betting on horse races or other sporting events, lotteries, bingo, roulette, slot machines, and more sophisticated games such as "playing" the futures grain market or stock market. These last two seem to be particularly attractive to professionals, including lawyers.

Obviously, many people who gamble do not develop a problem. But some researchers feel that pathological gambling in America is troubling, at the very least. Pathological gamblers often engage in destructive behaviors. They may commit crimes, run up large debts, and damage important relationships with family members and friends. There is a lack of basic research and wide consensus among scholars regarding statistics on gambling addiction, but the two principal studies sponsored by the National Research Council estimate that in a given year, approximately 1.8 million adults in the United States are pathological gamblers.[1]

Compulsive gambling is a progressive disorder in which the individual has a psychologically uncontrollable preoccupation with gambling. The problem gambler may become obsessed with an overwhelming urge to gamble and, without intervention, will continue down a path of destruction, similar to alcohol and other drug addiction. The primary symptoms are emotional dependence on gambling, loss of control, and continued interference with any of the major life areas such as health, occupation, relationships, spirituality, and financial health.

All addictive diseases operate in the same area of the brain. Substance addictions and process addictions use different pathways, but a tendency to have one type of addiction may make us more susceptible to other addictions. A study reported in December 2001 by the University at Buffalo's Research Institute on Addictions found problem drinkers were twenty-three times more likely to have a gambling problem than those who were not heavy drinkers. This same study found that compulsive gambling is significantly higher among minorities and lower-income individuals. The study also stated that when individuals from higher socioeconomic groups became compulsive gamblers, they were more likely to become alcohol dependent than lower-income individuals.[2]

Compulsive gambling is often characterized by three stages:

1. the search for action or the winning phase
2. the chase or the losing phase
3. the desperation phase

The action-seeking phase is a way of life in which risk taking and thrill seeking are very important. Gambling is both fun and exciting. It is normal to have some wins to offset the losses and enough "big wins" to convince the gambler of the potential for becoming rich through gambling. But continued gambling leads to increased losses of both money and self-esteem. To regain these, the gambler borrows money and bets on credit and then has to borrow more money to cover the new losses. Despite the occasional big win, the reality is that the gambler is going to continue to lose in the long run. The gambler begins to hide how much is being borrowed and lost and spends more time gambling in the chase to break even.

The gambling behavior intensifies as financial, personal, and professional problems multiply. The preoccupation with gambling begins to dominate the gambler's life in a vain attempt to regain money and respect. This downward progression can last for years, resulting in extraordinary losses of productive time and money. Unless treated, the gambling addiction often will reach the point where it compromises, disrupts, and then destroys the gambler's personal and professional lives. These problems further aggravate the gambling behavior. This is the desperation phase as the problem gambler becomes obsessed with breaking even and paying off debts. The betting is often done with borrowed or stolen money and may be triggered by a large loss and subsequent losses.

A vicious and destructive cycle is in place that leads to desperate acts of lying, stealing, writing bad checks, embezzlement, fraudulent loan applications, secret loans, falsified expense accounts, alcohol or other drug abuse, severe mood swings (including anxiety and depression), and contemplation of and attempts at suicide. At some point all of the options run out except for suicide, running away, prison, or getting help from an addiction treatment professional.

Many compulsive gamblers are unable to ask for help, and it becomes the responsibility of family members or friends to take action through an intervention. If an intervention becomes necessary, remember that an intervention works best when properly planned and conducted by an addiction treatment professional.

CHAPTER SIXTEEN

Cocaine

Old Attitudes and New Dangers—
How Changing Attitudes Have Affected
Societal Use of a Dangerous Drug

MORE AMERICANS USE ALCOHOL than any other drug.[1] Alcohol use is responsible for thousands of fatalities each year, but there is another drug that is having a profound effect, both on how we think about chemical dependency and on addiction treatment. In the 1980s and early 1990s, cocaine became the "in drug" in certain social circles for lawyers, and it's still a problem today. In 2004, an estimated 2 million Americans aged twelve and older were current cocaine users, and 5.6 million used the drug during the last year (twelve months previous to the survey).[2]

Cocaine was first isolated from the South American coca leaf, as its most active alkaloid, in the 1880s by Albert Niemann. Coca-Cola's original Coke was marketed as a patent medicine and contained cocaine. Coca-Cola abandoned the use of cocaine in its syrup in 1903, but many respected health professionals, not to mention President William McKinley, praised cocaine as a medical wonder drug. Cocaine was first regulated in the United States in 1914 and continues to be used medically as local anesthesia for certain operations. But after it was initially lauded as a medical breakthrough and given fashionable credibility by Sherlock Holmes's use in the literary world, cocaine generally disappeared from the scene in the 1920s and 1930s and was considered a drug of great depravity used only in the roughest urban ghettos.

This changed during the late 1960s and early 1970s when cocaine emerged from the ghetto and again obtained a degree of respectability in certain circles. At this time, many health professionals and substance abuse treatment centers sent mixed messages to the public about cocaine. Some viewed cocaine as "safe" because its use did not seem to have all of the classic medical symptoms of other addictive drugs. For example, cocaine use did not promote tolerance to a great degree, and withdrawal from cocaine did not appear to be nearly as dangerous as withdrawal from drugs such as heroin or alcohol. Users of cocaine often inhaled the powder form into their nostrils where it was carried into the bloodstream through the tiny blood vessels in the nose's mucous membrane.

Then the practice of freebasing began, which involved inhaling a highly concentrated form of cocaine vapor directly into the lungs. This type of use brought death and other tragedies. Professional opinion altered dramatically, and cocaine rapidly came to be viewed as a very dangerous drug. At the same time, cocaine became a prestigious drug with an elite reputation, and its market began to expand rapidly as cocaine became both much cheaper and much stronger. This increased usage also brought a dramatic increase in cocaine-related medical emergencies and fatalities.

In 1985, a new form of freebase cocaine called "crack" appeared on the East Coast and began spreading across the country. Crack is a form of cocaine hydrochloride that is processed into a resulting powder or crystals known as "rocks." It is thought that the name crack comes from the crackling sound made when the drug is smoked. The crystals are white and are about the size of pencil erasers. Crack became available on street corners in ready-to-smoke form at a price of around five to ten dollars a rock. The development of crack was a marketing coup on the same scale as the sliced loaf of bread or the disposable ink pen. It made the drug ready for immediate use, available at prices that the youth market could afford, and allowed for ingestion by smoking. Cocaine, in any form, affects the electrical signals sent between the brain and the heart and can cause potentially fatal seizures. Although it is now very clear that cocaine use is a potentially fatal activity, many users continue to see use through the attitudes of proceeding decades, when the risk seemed minimal.

What do lawyers and other individuals need to know about the dangers of crack? First, it is important to understand why crack is so highly

addictive. When crack is smoked, it reaches the brain almost instanta-
neously, providing a very quick "high." The crack high does not last
long, however, and is usually followed by a profound "low" that leaves
the user depressed, agitated, and craving more cocaine to eliminate the
symptoms of the low. Because the crack high is so intense and pleasurable but short, crack users take the drug again and again to relive the
original high. As a result, the addictive process with crack seems to accelerate in the body.

The person who is a relatively short-time crack user may experience
the same level of addictive disease that affects an alcoholic who has been
drinking heavily for twenty years. Many crack addicts express the belief
that their addiction started with first-time use. Some brain chemistry research indicates that cocaine, in any form, increases the release of naturally occurring, pleasure-inducing brain chemicals, such as dopamine,
while at the same time reducing the brain's ability to reprocess these
components. The inevitable result is the familiar downward spiral of
addiction.

Medically, we now know much more about the effects of cocaine
than have been known in the past. Cocaine increases the blood pressure
markedly, which can cause fatal brain hemorrhaging as blood acceler-
ates through arteries at a much greater pace. Another source of cocaine
fatalities comes from the changes that occur in the heartbeat as the electrical signal between the brain and the heart becomes distorted. As the
heartbeat speeds up above its normal rate, the heart may skip beats and
then double up on contractions.

Cocaine can have an effect on skin coloration, causing the skin to
have a yellow or grayish cast, probably because of damage to the liver. It
also stimulates the oil glands in the skin, often causing pimples and acne.

Cocaine users often suffer from bronchitis and coughing. Cocaine
affects the membranes of the openings to the lungs, causing the forma-
tion of mucous and inflammation. Another symptom of cocaine use is
an overstimulation of muscle fibers, which causes involuntary contractions. This may result in cocaine users having facial tics or involuntary
jerks of the body caused by faulty signals going to muscle fibers. The
electrical misfiring caused by cocaine has resulted in convulsions.

Emotionally, cocaine users ride a roller coaster of extreme highs in
which they feel powerful and in control, followed by extreme lows in

which they feel irritable, suspicious, and depressed. The emotional effects of cocaine are likely to be seen most readily in the disruption of the family system. Lawyers addicted to cocaine often have strained relationships with other law partners or associates. These addicts may also suffer from financial problems as a result of the high cost of sustaining the cocaine habit.

The evidence is absolutely clear that cocaine, which was once viewed as a wonderful medical discovery, with effects so beneficial that it could be an ingredient in a popular soft drink, is in fact a dangerous and vicious drug. The difficulty is that the general population may be viewing cocaine through the eyes of an earlier generation and through the ambivalence of medical and treatment professionals ten to twenty years ago. We do not need to be re-educated the hard way. Cocaine hooks users quickly and significantly alters brain chemistry. Ignoring cocaine addiction does not make it go away. Cocaine is usually used in conjunction with alcohol. This may accelerate the brain chemistry changes that make a person dependent upon alcohol. In fact, cross-addiction with alcohol is almost always inevitable. Cocaine addiction only gets worse. Because cocaine is so destructive, the addict should immediately seek help from a professional addiction treatment counselor.

CHAPTER SEVENTEEN

Sleep Disorders

Sleep Problems May Be a Predictor of Alcohol Problems

ONE OF THE GREAT BENEFITS and burdens of technology has been the increase of demands on our time. As time pressures increase, so does stress. Even fun activities can become stressful when we are worried about being late to the next appointment. The lawyer's day is often just one mad scramble with the clock. The stress of keeping up with an external clock must be understood in the context of our own internal clock.

We all have internal software that programs us to anticipate and prepare for changes in the physical environment that are associated with day and night. Researchers in the field of chronobiology are addressing these mechanisms, including our biological timekeeping system. Research in this area often focuses on the daily cycle known as circadian rhythm. The term "circadian" derives from the Latin phrase *circa diem* which means "about a day." In mammals, the circadian clock resides primarily in two clusters of nerve cells called the suprachiasmatic nuclei (SCN) located at the base of the brain in the anterior hypothalamus.

Sleep problems are often more common among alcoholics and other drug addicts than among non-addicts. During periods of withdrawal, recovering people commonly experience problems falling asleep and decreased total sleep time. Even individuals who have been abstinent for extended periods of time may continue to experience persistent sleep abnormalities.

For some individuals, insomnia may be a precursor of alcoholism. Individuals, including lawyers, commonly use alcohol to self-medicate for insomnia, and this may be part of the reason that insomnia seems to precede the onset of alcoholism among some individuals. Many active alcoholics seem to use alcohol to help induce sleep prior to entering treatment. Individuals in recovery may still have difficulties with sleep, which can increase their chances of relapse.

Even the timing of alcohol consumption may be influenced considerably by the circadian rhythm. The brain's use of alcohol has a complex effect on the human circadian rhythm, including effecting changes in the level of REM sleep, body temperature, and cortisol and melatonin release. While chronobiology research is still relatively new, enough has been learned to suggest that some of alcohol's negative health consequences may be related to a disruption of the normal timing pattern in which our bodies function.

Sleep is also a very important factor related to depression because of the point in the sleep cycle in which serotonin production is replenished. Serotonin is the neurotransmitter that causes a feeling of well-being. During the last phase of sleep there is an increase in serotonin and in the delta and theta brain waves, which are particularly restorative to the body. The problem is that when sleep is interrupted, this last cycle must start all over. In addition, certain chemicals often taken to relax, such as alcohol and prescription tranquilizers such as Xanax and Valium, actually depress phase four of the sleep cycle. Similarly, more than five hundred milligrams of caffeine (from coffee and soft drinks) in any twenty-four-hour period will also tend to prevent stage-four sleep.

If an individual is sleeping eight hours a night but not waking up feeling good, chances are something is preventing a restorative phase four in his or her sleep. Being able to get a good night's sleep is an important marker of good health. Not sleeping well is often a complex symptom that should be discussed with a health care provider who understands depression and addiction.

Understanding Depression

CHAPTER EIGHTEEN

Preventing Suicide in Lawyers

Understanding the Link between Addiction and Depression

MORE AMERICANS die every year from suicide than from homicide.[1] Unlike the elaborate justice system, with its guaranteed right of appeal for the defendant and a public process for reconciling the societal effects of homicide, we have developed no system to prevent, understand, and reconcile suicide and its aftermath.

Of course, this is not just a problem of the legal profession, but some statistical data suggest that lawyers are more at risk for suicide than other professions or vocations.[2] Between 1984 and 1993 the local Charlotte, North Carolina, Bar experienced eight suicides in nine years. Lawyers are prone to the diseases of addiction and depression that can lead to suicide. In addition, lawyers and other professionals in the justice system often carry a heavy emotional burden from knowing the details of homicides and other crimes against individuals and society.

Substance abuse and depression are two underlying conditions that can often lead a person to commit suicide. Both of these underlying conditions can either be prevented or mitigated by timely intervention and treatment to prevent a suicide from occurring. As lawyers, we need to know how to recognize the signs and symptoms of a lawyer at risk for suicide, and know how to get help.

The Depressed Lawyer

Depression is a disabling disorder that involves feeling more than "blue" or "sad" when a challenging event has occurred. A clinical diagnosis of depression (which can range from mild to severe) requires a depressed mood or lack of interest in everyday activities for at least two weeks, plus at least four of the following symptoms:

- a change in appetite or weight
- an inability to sleep or sleeping too much
- slowed or restless movement
- reduced energy
- difficulty concentrating or making decisions
- feelings of guilt or worthlessness
- thoughts of death or suicide

These symptoms must be severe enough to interfere with the ordinary functioning of life. Individuals suffering from depression often become discouraged, don't eat a healthy diet, and don't exercise. Depressed individuals may be more prone to use addictive substances to deal with feelings of sadness and isolation.

Because lawyers are involved in helping others, they often have little awareness of their own needs and emotional issues. Often the depressed lawyer, like the alcoholic, does not realize that he or she has an illness. Over time, a depressed state of being becomes the norm. The depressed lawyer is unable to face normal routine tasks at work, while his or her view of the world becomes increasingly narrow, negative, and limited. Depression can occur on its own or as a co-occurring disorder along with alcohol or other drug addiction.

The Alcoholic Lawyer

Addiction to alcohol is a brain disease. Predisposition to alcoholism often runs in families. The continuous use of alcohol causes the parts of the brain that create the normal "feel-good" neurotransmitters to shut down. While most individuals use alcohol to experience an elevation in mood, or to feel "better than normal," the alcoholic is ingesting alcohol just to feel "normal." But this alcohol-induced feeling of normalcy becomes more and more elusive as alcoholism progresses. In addition to the skewed brain chemistry caused by alcoholism, the alcoholic eventually may experience tremendous guilt and remorse as he or she is no longer able to function normally and as his or her behavior again and again disappoints himself or herself and others. The normal state for an alcoholic is often depression fueled by fear, guilt, and anger.

As alcoholism progresses, the alcoholic lawyer loses meaningful relations with family members, friends, and co-workers. By the time the lawyer has nothing in life but a job, there is not much left of value to live for. Depression often makes suicidal thoughts more common. Among alcoholic lawyers who commit suicide, a major factor is often public disclosure of addiction, wrongs committed while intoxicated, or disbarment.

Signs of Alcoholism and Depression

Although there are certain specific symptoms for alcoholism and depression, many of the outward signs are similar for both diseases. The symptoms of alcoholism and depression include:

- feeling depressed, sad, or anxious during most of the day
- neglecting the family and losing interest in activities
- changes in weight
- changes in sleep patterns
- feeling less energy
- financial difficulties
- a general increase in health problems
- feelings of worthlessness and guilt
- isolation from friends and family
- reduced ability or inability to concentrate

If a lawyer seems to suffer from addiction along with another co-occurring disorder, such as depression or anxiety, he or she should have a comprehensive physical examination to identify any separate conditions, such as thyroid disease or diabetes, which might be contributing to the problem. Second, the lawyer should see a psychiatrist who is certified by the American Society of Addiction Medicine (ASAM). This assures that the treating physician understands both addiction and depression and their interaction. Depending on the situation, the psychiatrist may prescribe antidepressants, which can significantly help some individuals with depression.

CHAPTER NINETEEN

Grandiosity, Injustice, and Depression
Identifying Causes of Depression in Lawyers

THERE MAY BE A POTENTIAL LINK between the increase in depression among lawyers and the problem of world injustice. Robert Moore, a Jungian psychologist and a professor at the Chicago Theological Seminary, has performed research on the cultural causes of harm in our collective psyches. Moore's book *Facing The Dragon: Confronting Personal and Spiritual Grandiosity* is an extraordinary step forward in trying to understand these cultural issues.

Moore asks some hard questions. Where does societal harm come from? Why, in our modern secular society, do we tend to deny examining the psychological underpinnings of injustice? In denying the reality of what creates injustice in the world, do we give it power? Moore finds that the answer is portrayed in J. R. R. Tolkien's *The Lord of the Rings* series, where a lust for power grows until it threatens to destroy the entire world. This fantasy masterpiece, Moore believes, reflects a process that is active not just in "Middle-earth," but also on planet Earth.

Perhaps the core issue for each of us, personally and collectively as a community, involves how we deal with the powerful grandiose energies that burn in every human heart, which seek to make us more godlike. We may not be aware of grandiosity's presence, but often it is manifesting in our lives in ways to avoid our very humanness. Typically, we either identify with grandiosity or we repress it and project it onto others.

First, grandiosity can present itself in humans through posturing and pretension to assert more control in their lives than is possible. In this pattern, people may be addicted to the idealizing projections and energy of other people. An individual may even feel that he or she is above the law—the law is for others, not him or her.

Second, grandiosity presents itself in workaholics, in the fantasy that they can keep the world from crashing down around themselves by working harder and harder. Lawyers often feel a self-righteousness that their work, efforts, and views of the world are necessary for justice to be done. They see the wrong to be righted, the need for which they are the instrument of justice. This form of grandiosity enables them to act without empathy, compassion, or love.

The third form of grandiosity is being emotionally "above it all." An individual may think that he or she is always right and only he or she has the enlightened point of view. If people would only accept and follow the individual's version of truth, everything would be okay. The individual uses this to avoid any responsibility for confronting challenging things happening in the world. This grandiose fantasy allows the individual to reject any notion of cooperating with others with compassion and justice.

A fourth form of grandiosity is a person's belief that the world begins and ends with his or her feelings, pain, and bodily and emotional needs. The person believes his or her needs are great and that people don't give them the importance they deserve. The person's victimization becomes the most important thing in the world. Everyone else is at fault but him or her. Others created this hell he or she is living, and others should work to get him or her out of it. If the others were really adequate and responsible, they would liberate the individual from his or her pain and suffering and provide him or her with more food, narcotics, sex, money, and status.

The common aspects of unconscious grandiosity are chronic anxiety; despair; depression; hopelessness; aimlessness; lack of a sense of limits; lack of a sense of mystery; emotional coldness ranging from detachment to hate; and a lack of empathy, compassion, or joy. The more unconscious grandiosity a person has, the more anxiety he or she experiences.

Jungian studies suggest that we are all part of a larger collective unconscious. It makes sense to think that our own issues of personal grandiosity, which are not dealt with individually, go into the collective unconsciousness in a way that constellates injustice. When this occurs, unfairness results.

What is the solution? What can lawyers do with their individual grandiose energies? Programs of recovery are designed to help deflate the grandiose ego. Engaging in conversations with God, or a Higher Power, can prevent grandiose energies from inflating someone's ego. Therapy may be a solution. For some individuals who cannot afford to go to therapy or counseling, the regular ritual process provided by traditional religious services may be a container that helps regulate the volatility of an individual's emotions.

CHAPTER TWENTY

Beyond Relief

Helping Lawyers Achieve True Healing
from Depression

THERE HAS BEEN A RECENT REVOLUTION in public attitude about the use of antidepressant medication. In the past few years, antidepressant medication ads have become as common in the media as ads for beer or Viagra. In the 1991 North Carolina Bar Association Quality-of-Life Survey, only 3 percent of the lawyers polled reported that they were taking antidepressant medication. The 2003 follow-up survey by the North Carolina Chief Justice's Commission on Professionalism reported that 16.8 percent of the lawyers polled were using prescription medication for anxiety and/or depression. This is an increase of 13.8 percent in twelve years. When the initial 1991 survey was conducted, many of the Bar Association leaders were afraid that lawyers who were depressed were not getting medical attention or, if appropriate, pharmacological treatment.

There are still lawyers who suffer from depression who are not getting the help they need. But today, there is a large segment of lawyers who are taking antidepressant medication. Some of these lawyers may feel relief from depressive symptoms because of the prescription medication they are receiving—but these lawyers have often not been able to address the underlying causes of their depression. In fact, the use of the antidepressant may have allowed them to avoid facing emotional pain or challenging feelings, which could allow healing to begin. Medicating depression may allow individuals relief so they no longer have the motivation to get therapy or counseling to discover and heal the underlying causes of depression. These people are in a kind of psychic limbo where their pain is medicated, but they have not regained a full emotional life.

Often a psychiatrist will provide prescription medication for depression, which can significantly help some patients. But medication is, at best, a partial treatment. Any person suffering from depression who is not under the care of a counselor or therapist may not be fully addressing his or her depression. The difficulty arises when psychiatrists do not perform counseling or therapy, but rather perform as "medication managers." Many patients would rather just take a pill than engage in counseling. Whether an individual uses antidepressant medication or not, counseling is often necessary in order to truly identify the source of depression and promote thorough and enduring healing.

Many individuals who use antidepressants do not receive counseling for depression. Dr. David Burns, a psychiatrist on the faculty at Stanford, started his career as a neuropharmacologist, studying treatment of mental disorders with prescription medications. Eventually Burns came to believe that new therapeutic techniques such as cognitive behavioral therapy were very effective, often more than antidepressants, for helping people heal from depression.[1]

The underlying premise of cognitive behavioral therapy is that if you change how you think, you'll change how you feel. What Dr. Burns and other researchers have discovered is that underlying most depressive states are self-destructive negative thoughts and beliefs that an individual possesses about himself or herself. These self-destructive beliefs are often not true, but cause the individual to have a negative self-image.

There are several key components that can allow us to heal from depression. First, if the depression is debilitating, pharmacological treatment can help. Second, therapy can help recognize and heal underlying emotional issues that may be causing depression. Third, support group participation can break down the isolation in which depression thrives. Fourth, good exercise and nutrition can help alleviate the symptoms of depression.

Social support is a simple but powerful weapon against depression. I recommend that lawyers suffering from depression participate on a weekly basis with others to whom they can talk openly and frankly. Twelve Step groups such as Emotions Anonymous or Depression Anonymous may be particularly helpful. In many states, Lawyer Assistance Programs (LAPs) facilitate support groups for lawyers with depression.

Exercise and diet are also extremely important in treating depression. Exercise appears to increase the levels of serotonin in the body. Exercise is also one of the most effective ways to rid the body of the buildup of chemical agents caused by stress. Individuals suffering from depression should avoid alcohol, caffeine, and sugar, which may give temporary highs, but can worsen the symptoms of depression.

Lawyers who feel depressed should follow these general guidelines:

- Address the issue sooner rather than later.
- Seek evaluation from a physician and an ASAM-certified psychiatrist.
- Use prescription medication where appropriate, but don't let it be the sole treatment of this disorder.
- Obtain cognitive behavioral therapy from a licensed professional.
- Exercise.
- Utilize good nutrition.
- Participate in a weekly self-help program of social support.

Depression can affect an individual's beliefs and attitudes and can cause an individual to perceive his or her life in a narrow, confined way. To begin to heal, develop these three important attitudes.

1. Honesty: Self-honesty is necessary to see the nature of depression clearly and to identify feelings, expectations, and attitudes about it.
2. Openness: Openness involves accepting the limited way in which we have viewed the disease of depression and being open to treatment methods.
3. Willingness: We must be willing to take action to heal from all aspects of depression. Making positive changes can change our attitude and allows us to accept depression and heal from it.

Individuals seeking true recovery from depression should put these three attitudes to work in his or her relationships. We can all benefit when we foster those relationships that are healing—those that bring out our best, allow acceptance of our worth, and put our worth to useful service.

These proactive steps are not hard to do; in fact, exercise, good nutrition, attitude, and social support are a part of any program of good health, but often these elements have been neglected, and their neglect is part of what has led to depression. Depression is like most diseases—the sooner it receives proper medical treatment, the greater the chance of remission and the better the long-term prognosis.

Treatment Works

The good news is that treatment is available for both alcoholism and depression. As with all diseases, the longer alcoholism and depression go untreated, the greater the likelihood of developing other concurrent problems and the greater the likelihood of suicide. Because depression and alcoholism are both chronic, long-term diseases, there is a need for ongoing support that focuses on preventing isolation and increasing the following: (a) physical activity to increase endorphins, (b) intellectual activity, (c) social activity, and (d) spiritual activity.

What to Do When a Lawyer Needs Help

Lawyers must take suicide as seriously as the law profession takes homicide. More lives are lost to suicide than to homicide, and the cost to suicide survivors—friends and family members of suicide victims—is very high. Suicide is a phenomenon that tends to perpetuate itself in families. Once a family member commits suicide there is a much greater risk that other family members will follow. The highest rates of suicide are for single or widowed men over fifty-five.[2]

Many lawyers feel uncomfortable helping another lawyer, even one they know well, who may be suffering from the danger of suicide. This is often because these lawyers do not know how to help. However, it is our duty, as professional colleagues, to bring confidential help to other lawyers who we feel are at risk for suicide.

If you feel a lawyer is in immediate danger of suicide, call 911 to summon help. In a nonemergency situation call your state's Lawyer Assistance Program, which can be found by calling the American Bar Association's Commission on Lawyer Assistance Programs at 312-988-5359. Additionally, the number for the National Suicide Prevention Lifeline is 1-800-273-TALK (8255). The mission of the National Suicide Prevention Lifeline is to provide immediate assistance to individuals in suicidal crisis by connecting them to the nearest crisis center in their area.

CHAPTER TWENTY-ONE

Kitchen Table Friends

Freedom from Emotional Isolation as a Path to Healing

TWO MALE LAWYERS who were very respected members of the Bar were both being treated by the same counselor. Each lawyer entered counseling because of loneliness, depression, and burnout. Neither man was aware that the other was also seeking help. As the separate sessions progressed, both men talked about their deep compassion for many of their clients and of their love of the law. When these lawyers lost a case they would often share their feelings with the counselor and discuss how the loss felt. Similar to individuals in other professions, these lawyers were taught to look at each client's case objectively. These lawyers felt that expressing grief about their own personal loss, or a loss incurred by a client, was unprofessional or even unmanly. Experiencing these emotions, but not sharing them, often left the lawyers feeling lonely and isolated.

In the safety of the counselor's office these two lawyers began to wonder out loud about their feelings, about their work, and about their impact on the lives of their clients. They often shared stories about their clients' cases with great animation. The two men had been professional partners for more than twenty years. They shared a receptionist, a staff of paraprofessionals, and an office, but they didn't really know each other. They unknowingly shared a counselor (who was ethically bound not to tell either about the other's visits or even that they were both patients). The counselor encouraged each to talk with the other partner about these feelings, but the counselor got the same response each time: "Him? Heavens, he would just laugh."

Lawyers often feel isolated from others by the nature of their work experiences. The attorney-client privilege prevents us from talking with those outside our firms about client matters. Within our firms, it is just as difficult to talk to each other about our feelings and experiences. Many lawyers have been socialized to believe that it is scientific objectivity that makes them most effective in their efforts to understand and resolve a client's problems. Lawyers often adopt a mental distance to protect themselves from becoming wounded by the moral and ethical conflicts that arise in their work. Law school is demanding training. Yet objectivity leaves us far more emotionally vulnerable than compassion or simple humanity. Objectivity separates us from the life around us and within us. We are wounded by life just the same; it only separates us so that healing cannot reach us. In the objective stance, we can't draw on our individual human strengths, cry, accept comfort, find meaning, or pray.

The ability to let go of objectivity and be fully present with a client is more a matter of cultivating a sense of perspective and meaning about life. It is more a spiritual quality than a mental one. We can start to cultivate presence by becoming more present to ourselves and to others. First, we should take time to experience our feelings and then find someone who will listen without judgment. Many lawyers benefit from a guided structure, often provided by a good counselor or through a self-help group, that helps address major life issues. Normal depression (as opposed to clinical depression where the assistance of a psychiatrist is needed) can be the natural way the psyche heals by pushing us inward to face an emotional rigidity that has taken the joy and enthusiasm out of life.

An impulse to pursue wholeness is natural and exists in all of us, though each of us heals in our own way. Some people heal because they have work to do. Others heal because they have been released from their work and the pressures and expectations that others place on them. Some people need music, while others need humor. Across the board, all individuals need to be freed from their own emotional isolation in order to find healing and joy in their lives. We need to be able to share our experiences over the kitchen table. It is not what is said during these conversations as much as the process of sharing that brings wisdom.

Understanding the Solutions

CHAPTER TWENTY-TWO

Attitude and Disease

Helping Lawyers Adopt Attitudes
That Promote Healing

MEDICINE AND SCIENCE are naturally biased toward trying to understand the cause of disease. Doctors want a diagnosis. But with many chronic illnesses and mental health disorders, a diagnosis is no more than a collection of identified symptoms. Ultimately, it does not matter how much of an individual's depression, alcoholism, or other drug addiction is genetic or environmentally predisposed. What is important is learning how to heal. The lawyers who get better—the ones who heal from chronic illness—are those lawyers who stay focused on the solutions.

One of the great issues being debated in the healing arts is whether our thoughts and attitudes influence illness and if so, how. This inquiry raises two questions. First, is the risk for acquiring a physical disease increased by depression or a negative outlook on life? Second, when an individual has a disease, does having a positive emotional outlook enhance his or her chance of recovery?

Numerous studies have looked at whether personality or mood has an influence in preventing cancer or in promoting the onset of cancer. These studies suggest that emotional disorders do not appear to have a significant impact on the rate at which cancer occurs in the general population. However, there are two huge exceptions. Of all the ailments listed in the American Psychiatric Association's *Diagnostic and Statistical Manual of Mental Disorders,* two directly affect the body and mental outlook and increase the risk of cancer: nicotine dependence and alcohol dependence.

There is a correlation between individuals who are nicotine or alcohol dependent and depression. People with alcohol and nicotine dependency are more likely to be depressed, and people with a history of depression are more likely to abuse alcohol and more likely to smoke cigarettes. People with depression are also less likely to quit smoking once they start.

Many of us have known individuals whose positive outlook on life seemed to help them deal with a serious physical illness, but overall the studies suggest that a patient's attitude has little effect on the onset of the physical part of a disease such as cancer. However, once a serious illness has been contracted, emotional outlook *does* affect the outcome of cancer in the same way it affects the outcome of other illnesses. Some of the reasons for this are obvious. People with low morale are less likely to take good care of themselves. In addition, some studies of the impact of stress hormones on the immune system show that positive thinkers are less damaged by stress than negative thinkers. Both depression and chronic stress cause long-term overexposure to the adrenal hormones epinephrine and cortisol. The continued production of these stress-response neurochemicals in the body tends to depress the immune system.

The National Cancer Institute is sponsoring ongoing research to evaluate the relationship between the mind and the immune system, and the impact of this relationship on patients suffering from cancer. Once a serious illness is contracted, psychotherapy and support groups can greatly enhance the lives of the affected patients by reducing stress, relieving depression, and alleviating the tendency to isolate. In addition to support groups, other techniques such as biofeedback, muscle relaxation, hypnosis, and guided imagery also use the mind's influence to reduce the stress reaction in the body. The importance of group support and breaking down the barriers of isolation that a disease causes first came to light more than twenty years ago in a psychotherapy group study of women with breast cancer.[1] Prolonging the lives of the patients was not the original purpose of the study, so the researchers were surprised to discover that the women in the study who attended therapy groups survived, on average, almost twice as long as those in the control group (who did not attend therapy groups). After several years, all the patients in the control group had died, yet a third of the women in the support groups were still living.

The history of addiction treatment suggests a parallel to that of group support in cancer treatment. Addiction treatment emerged in the 1930s, from a time when there was no acknowledged medical intervention for the disease. Over the years, treatment for addiction for has shown that the support group aspect of Alcoholics Anonymous (AA) is extremely important to assure that the disease remains in remission. The support groups of AA help people find the coping skills to change patterns of behavior in their life that had become ingrained during use of alcohol or other drugs. It is much easier for individuals to develop new healthy patterns of behavior when engaged with others who understand and support healthy patterns rather than approaching the changes alone.

The experience of recovering alcoholics and other addicts in support groups generally has helped answer one of the other intriguing questions about how attitude affects disease. How do we change our own negative thinking and negative attitudes? The founders of AA discovered that you don't change thinking by thinking. As Albert Einstein said, "The mind that created the problem doesn't solve it."

In other words, the way to change negative thought patterns is by taking positive actions in response to challenging emotions, such as fear, anxiety, or anger. Over time, the new actions will help the mind move to a more positive disposition. To take new, unaccustomed, positive actions, we need the support of others. This completes the circle for the efficacy of change that support groups can provide.

Studies concerning cancer support groups tend to show similar results to those of Twelve Step groups. It is often the new social support actions undertaken by patients that help bring them out of isolation and give them a more positive outlook on life. In turn, these positive outlooks motivate the patients to undertake positive activities that will help them endure their treatment and engage in healthy activities.

When Václav Havel was president of Czechoslovakia, he told the United States Congress that consciousness perceives being, not the other way around. Havel believed that the salvation of this human world lies nowhere else than in the human heart, in the human power to reflect, in human weakness, and in human responsibility.

What Václav Havel was saying about politics may also be true about disease. Matter is not the fundamental factor, rather consciousness is, or human awareness, or—if you prefer—spirituality. Those are the deeper sources of power with which people have been able to find healing on a cultural level that also engender healing on an individual level.

Through greater awareness, we have the opportunity to take new action where there is greater opportunity to heal ourselves. And in our work, in the law office each day, lawyers have the same opportunity to engender a positive atmosphere where there is more chance for wellness. Václav Havel suggests that it is the inner life and its vibrancy that ultimately helps create a healing and healthy outer life. Engaging a positive outlook will ultimately help enhance physical health, daily pursuits such as practicing law, and even community life. When the inner life is ignored, we can end up simply pushing ourselves harder and harder to get the job done each day. Efforts to create healing as a matter of outer arrangement, without working on inner well-being, will eventually destroy positive attitude, cause burnout, and lead to depression.

A healthy connection to ourselves, to others, and to something greater than ourselves is what nurtures our inner well-being. The cancer support group studies, the experience of Twelve Step groups, and Havel's comments all suggest that it is the quality of inner well-being that determines day-to-day emotional outlook and attitude. While this kind of positive disposition may not prevent disease from happening, the research results make clear that positive emotional outlook and attitude will increase survival rates when diseases do strike and make surviving not only possible, but something that can be done well.

CHAPTER TWENTY-THREE

Old Ideas and Stories

How Telling and Listening to Stories Can Transform Us

IN OBSERVING LAWYERS recover from addiction and depression, I see that healing physically and emotionally begins with giving up old ideas and adopting new ways of being. From the active alcoholic's perspective, the problem is not drinking, but not being *able* to drink. These individuals have told themselves stories such as "without alcohol, the irritation, fear, and the 'too high' volume of the world will not go away." Life can be richer and more joyful when individuals give up these stories, give up the need to be in control, and give up the illusion of control that alcohol and other drugs give.

Two old stories that addicted individuals need to let go of include:

1. I can drink alcohol again and not cause harm to my family and my own physical and emotional health.
2. Alcohol and other drugs have been the solution for most of my life. There are no other solutions.

Addicted people must not only let go of these old stories, they also must embrace new stories that demonstrate new possibilities in their lives. Telling and listening to stories is important to healing. And not just any story, but stories in which the teller and the listener(s) participate equally—stories in which there is participation without judgment.

The great teachers, such as Jesus and Buddha, taught by telling stories. The best trial lawyers know how to tell the story of their case to the jury in a way that makes it meaningful to them. For example, Fred Helms was senior partner at the firm where I first worked in Charlotte, North Carolina. Helms was known for his penchant for discourse. But in addition to his ability to harangue on and on about law, he was a wonderful storyteller.

When Prohibition came to Charlotte, North Carolina—as across the rest of the country—it brought to Charlotte those things that thrive with illegal activity, such as crime, gambling, and prostitution. Charlotte had "Cadillac Annie," the pride of the red-light district, and Basil "The Owl" Banghart, a mail-truck robber. Gambling was open in the form of slot machines.

Early on in his career as a lawyer, Helms was involved in civic enterprises to clean up Charlotte. One of his stories I liked best was about his defense of Frank Littlejohn, an unorthodox police detective whom the federal authorities had hired in the 1920s to infiltrate the Ku Klux Klan in South Carolina. Littlejohn eventually became Charlotte's chief of police, but because of his tendency to pay little attention to police department rules, he was suspended from the force in 1940. Helms took on Littlejohn's case pro bono. Along with Frank N. Kennedy and Elmer Hilker, Helms defended Littlejohn in an appeal before the Civil Service Commission. The hearing lasted five weeks. Helms cross-examined the police chief for three days. Helms could reminisce about the Littlejohn case with a fascination that kept me caught up in a world as real as the one I actually knew.

Helms's account of those events taught me how much storytelling can move people out of believing their old ideas. Whether the founders of AA knew this or whether storytelling simply developed as a natural part of the Twelve Step principle of self-honesty, there is no way of knowing. What we do know is that storytelling works. When an alcoholic tells his or her story about identifying the disease, how he or she initiated recovery, and what recovery is like, the alcoholic is able to change and to grow. When individuals listen to the stories of others in recovery, the listeners discover the possibility of letting go of old ideas to make room for needed change.

David Abram's remarkable book *The Spell of the Sensuous* presents a compelling argument of how written language has estranged the human and nonhuman world. His book reminds me of the saying that every advance of science carries with it an equal loss. For as much as we have benefited from knowledge being advanced and disseminated by the printed word, Abram demonstrates how, in the process, wisdom has been lost. While Abram is particularly concerned about how the abstraction of written language has estranged us from the nonhuman world around us, his basic thesis is that we are open circuits that complete only when we are connected with others and with the encompassing earth.

Oral storytelling seems to be one way our circuitry gets completed as human creatures. Practical knowledge, moral patterns, social taboos, and the very language or manner of speech of any nonwriting culture are all maintained primarily through chants, myths, and legends—that is, through the telling of stories. Abram cites the example of the Apache culture where the use of *agodzaahi* tales—land-based narratives on humanity's relationship with the natural world—is part of the community fabric. When an Apache person offends the community by a certain act, one of his elders will, at an appropriate time (perhaps a community gathering), tell an appropriate *agodzaahi* story. The offender will not be identified or named aloud, but the listening offender "will feel the story penetrate deep beneath his skin."

While Abram emphasizes the importance of place and the nonhuman environment in the encompassing nature of stories, he leaves no doubt as to the importance that oral stories have had on the human psyche for thousands of years. While I can use printed words to tell you an interesting, even entertaining, story, I cannot in writing, nor can you as a reader, participate with that story in quite the same way as if I were telling you the story orally.

The steps that make healing and recovery from chronic diseases such as alcoholism and depression possible are pretty simple—not easy, but simple. To recover means letting go of old ideas. One often begins with stories, first as a listener to stories of those who have traveled the same path, and eventually as an individual sharing his or her story with others who may have no other way to break free of their old ideas. Telling these stories is a pretty simple idea and a simple process that's been wired into our brains for thousands of years. This process offers an experience of understanding, an experience of wisdom, and an experience of who and what we are. It offers the opportunity for us to understand that no matter what we are caught in, we can become willing to change.

CHAPTER TWENTY-FOUR

Cave Paintings

How the Ancient Human Need for Oneness Can Heal

FOR THOUSANDS AND THOUSANDS OF YEARS humans were hunter-gatherers, and a few of the skills from that time period seem to be still programmed into many of us. Hunter-gatherers possessed quick, reactive alertness and aggressiveness when facing danger, which are also skills from which a good trial lawyer benefits. This hunter-gatherer "wiring" also drives us to escape our ordinary consciousness and plug into the collective consciousness of the world. Altered states of consciousness vary along a spectrum, but during the hunter-gatherer period the state that shamans valued was that of deep trance and hallucination. There are many ways that trance states are induced. One of the most well known and ancient is the use of psychotropic drugs. But other methods, just as effective, include those cultivated by mainstream religious traditions, such as meditation, fasting, singing and chanting, vigorous dancing, and rhythmic drumming. Religious mystics from many diverse traditions have used some or all of these methods as ways of changing their consciousness and achieving a state of ecstasy.

Like anything we humans do, there are both destructive and creative ways to achieve these altered states of consciousness. Daily use of alcohol teases the body with a brief feeling of mood elevation, but then actually hinders, by depressive affect, any meaningful spiritual journey.

In Paleolithic times, shamanism was not an addendum to human culture, it was an all-embracing way of life and thought. In our modern culture, the use of alcohol and other drugs is not an addendum, but has become a way of life for many. Maybe the lesson from those ancient cave painters is not to condemn those who have followed a spiritual impulse in a destructive manner, such as in abusing alcohol or other drugs to reach an altered state of consciousness, but instead to acknowledge this universal spiritual longing and to recognize that we can make a positive choice to realize our spiritual desire by communing with our Higher Power and with others who support recovery.

The cave painters can also tell us why recovery is not about religion, but instead about spirituality. In a sense, the cave painters solved the fundamental problem religions later came to face: how to create a theology that changes as people's experience of life changes. The cave painters held a theology of practice, not an ideological theology. It was the practice of rituals that allowed them to have transcendent religious experiences. These experiences were kept alive and invoked by the images on the cave walls.

Unlike ideas, the meaning of images can change from individual to individual, and can change as his or her understanding of life grows and needs change. The individuals I know who have active, meaningful spiritual lives tell me that their understanding of God has changed significantly over the years, and often dramatically during a time of crisis. But for many of these people, the images that contain their connection to their spiritual aspect have stayed the same. Images such as those of the Buddha, the cross, or the black Madonna illustrate how powerfully images can connect people in a spiritual way without the fetters of ideology.

In addition to the physiological addiction that an alcoholic suffers (cravings, for example), there is often among lawyers—whether chemically addicted or not—an underlying psychological addiction to power and control. Breaking the physical craving requires addressing the underlying psychological need.

Part of the great wisdom of Twelve Step recovery is that it has no ideology. In our modern world full of visual images, it is probably good that, unlike the cave painters' images, Twelve Step recovery does not rely on visual images. But it does follow the cave painters' idea of a theology of practice, not of ideology. The Twelve Steps incorporate the universal practices of prayer, meditation, forgiveness, and gratitude to deal with the soul sickness and devastation that the disease of addiction brings and to open up the possibility of transcendent change.

I have a friend in recovery who told me that that his teenager asked him how praying for someone could be telling God anything that God didn't already know. My friend replied to his teenager that prayer is a spiritual mystery that he didn't really understand. But what my friend did know is that the routine practice of prayer changes us, especially when we pray for someone we feel has wronged us. This frees us from the bondage of resentment that can keep us caught in the past and opens the opportunity to be fully present in life each day. In this way, a simple spiritual practice can return the same sense of awe and wonder to life that is seen in the long-ago paintings our ancestors made in caves.

CHAPTER TWENTY-FIVE

Hope

Understanding the Difficulties
and Opportunities of Hope

ONE OF THE MOST DIFFICULT ASPECTS of helping people struggling with alcoholism or depression is being able to bring them hope. We derive hope from hearing the experience of a recovering person and identifying with what happened during the course of that person's disease. We hope that if recovery happened for that person, perhaps it might also happen for us.

Hope is an emotion that can be very difficult for a person in the throes of active addiction, who often cannot imagine what it is like to experience well-being again. Similarly, it can be very difficult for an individual with a chronic disease, such as alcoholism or depression, who has achieved some relief, to have the vision or motivation to go further—to hope that he or she can really heal. Individuals in this position are often characterized as "stuck in relief." This describes the alcoholic who has somehow managed to stop drinking by going to AA meetings but is not working the Twelve Steps. He or she has achieved some relief but is not doing the work to deal with the underlying emotional issues that were being ignored through self-medication with alcohol or other drugs. For the depressed person, this is similar to taking antidepressant medication without addressing the underlying emotional issues that contributed to the depression.

Patients who are "stuck in relief" have to answer this question: "Do I just want to feel better, or do I want to get well?" To my knowledge, there are no clinical studies showing that antidepressant medication addresses the cause of depression. In fact, these medications are designed to treat the symptoms of depression, not the causes. Real recovery, from addiction or depression, requires the kind of opening up to emotions that is very hard for lawyers. Again, there is often the lack of hope that these lawyers can truly heal. These individuals think, "It's possible for others to feel joy, but not for me."

One reason hope is difficult at the "stuck-in-relief" stage is that many things in our culture represent the very neurotic illnesses we are trying to be free from. It seems that all we can hope for is to be neurotically adjusted to a neurotic society. If we looked at society as a clinical patient, we might come up with several diagnoses. We might just look at the ads for alcohol and conclude the patient was addicted. Or we might look at how many products are sold with sexual messages and easily determine that the patient is a sex or relationship addict. We could look at the work/life culture in law and easily conclude the patient has a work addiction. Maybe we look at how we treat our natural environment and conclude that the cultural patient is suffering from low self-esteem that creates dysthymia, which is a low-grade, longer-term depression.

The bottom line is that our popular culture does not give us much reason to recognize healthy patterns that can give us hope for personal change. To really recover from addiction or depression requires us to accept life on life's terms without avoiding how we feel. We must learn to develop the emotional capacity to come to terms with living in a world where we learn to love people who die, where there is much loss and sadness as well as joy.

Not only can we be "stuck in relief," we can also be stuck in creating our own solution. For those who have a chronic disease and find their life a struggle, this may mean buying self-help books or complaining about how law practice takes all of their time and then engaging in a time management course. Such attempts to remedy problems may help those without addictions but typically do not help individuals with chronic diseases.

People with severe addiction or depression may have no choice but to try to really get well. For these people, the hope of those who have gone before and recovered is essential. Our postmodern, materialistic, and reductionistic world offers few models for hope. When we deconstruct everything in a sort of linear cause and effect, we never find hope. But healing from chronic diseases does not occur in a linear Newtonian world. Healing is a process with many feedback loops of such complexity that it can be analogized to chaos theory.

The basis for chaos theory is nonlinear math developed in the nineteenth century by the French mathematician Jules Henri Poincaré who discovered that in complex systems there are points he call resonances. If an object in the system strays into a resonance point, the linear causal network determining the system no longer defines it. It is set free. This is why, despite gravity, sometimes meteors leave our solar system.

Hope and recovery from chronic disease is not rational. By engaging in the complex tasks of Twelve Step work, we are offered the chance for real recovery—to be set free. The road to the mountain doesn't cause the mountain to come into being but leads you to where it is.

When we get hope from the stories of others to stay on the road of recovery, to do the real work, then it is truly possible to enter that space where we can be set free, where healing occurs, and where life can again be joyful.

CHAPTER TWENTY-SIX

From Willful to Willing

How Our Will Can Keep Us Stuck or Help Us Heal

ONE OF THE GREAT CHANGES in our culture in recent history has been the shift in our understanding of will. Psychology has grown as a field with many varying schools of thought, but for the most part, the field does not discuss or consider the idea of will. Starting with Freud, will was repudiated as the prime mover, and instead the focus in psyche was on various motives, libido, and drives. The role of science has been, and is today, to help us understand these drives and urges, indeed to understand the very brain chemistry down to how the last molecule works.

Much of our scientific bent to reject will as a factor in understanding our psyches is a response to the Romantic movement's assertion of the individual. The romantic will's object was the assertion of personal individuality, if it could avoid the Scylla of megalomania and the Charybdis of guilt and despair. The preceding Enlightenment movement had rejected an approach that seemed to glorify individual whim.

More recent writers talk of two aspects of will as life force. The first is unconscious will, as seen in a small child who may be trying to pick up an object but be unaware that he or she has a goal—humanity before the Fall. The second is conscious will, the force of our conscious actions moving us toward a goal—humanity after the Fall. An example of conscious will would be: I learn math to graduate from high school so I can go to college. Of course, the line between what is consciously and unconsciously willed varies over time.

The problem of will lies in our recurring attempts to apply conscious will to those parts of our life where conscious will has no effect, and where this will becomes distorted under such coercion. Here are a few examples: I can will knowledge, but not wisdom; meekness, but not humility; bedtime, but not sleep; self-assertion, but not courage; religiosity, but not faith—and the list goes on and on.

One explanation of all our modern illnesses—of not feeling good enough, of anxiety and depression, and of addiction to substances and compulsive behavior—is because we are uncomfortable in our own skin. That is, we will what we are powerless to achieve alone. Frustration by such exertions of the will usually leads to more willfulness, which in turn heightens the frustration between what is sought and what cannot be gained.

The fact that we cannot necessarily will what we desire does not refute the concept of free will—but whether free or otherwise, the will is not sufficient by itself to gain the most sought human goals. It may be too broad a statement, but it seems to me all of our psychological and addictive problems come from trying to use our will to obtain relief from how we feel.

Happiness cannot be willed. Happiness comes out of a peculiar kind of relationship with our outer world—peculiar in the sense that we assert ourselves in it, but we are also open to having our external reality interpenetrate us (such as feeling grateful for a beautiful day or enjoying the gift of a hug from a friend). There is an expression that a child can be "too willful." This statement expresses the idea that overexertion of will is destructive both for the child and others.

So how does this discussion of will provide practical help? It may be that we can look closely at the use of our will and see if we are using it to move us into the stream of life, or to cause us to be caught in one spot swimming desperately upstream and going nowhere.

When we have problems living in the present, these are often problems of will. Are we using our will to try to live in the future? Are we waiting to start life after we will ourselves into law school, pass the Bar, get into a good job, get married, make partner, start a family, or retire? Or are we living in regret of the past—that we didn't try out for the law review, we didn't marry our first love, we couldn't have kids, we got a divorce, we lost our big case, or we won't be able to retire early? Either way, we are using our will to fight against our present life—by spending this precious time trying to control the future or by regretting the past.

Like any tool, willpower is useful only for certain things. Trying not to be chemically dependent, trying not to be depressed, or trying to make someone else happy by sheer force of will is similar to trying to pound a nail in with a saw. You cannot succeed using willpower on issues over which it has little effect.

On the other hand, willingness denotes openness to a world full of discovery and to mystery. Willingness is a necessary attitude to confronting the joy and sorrow of living—experiencing its losses and fullness. Willingness allows us to explore what is really under our control—not much except our own approach to life—and to simultaneously accept that most of the universe lies forever outside of our ability to influence by force. Establishing a realistic relationship with our will is a primary task for a happy life and a necessity for anyone seeking to recover from a long-term chronic disease. Usually the key is to move from willfulness to a more conscious level of willingness—to be more open to the discovery that our lives may be vastly richer if we are open to wisdom and meaning outside ourselves.

CHAPTER TWENTY-SEVEN

Stuck

How to Take an Emotional Inventory

RECENTLY, social scientists have taken a look at the relationship between material well-being and emotional well-being, or happiness. For most of the world, greater levels of material wealth have led to greater levels of perceived emotional well-being—most everywhere, that is, but in the United States.[1] In the United States, the number of people defining themselves as "very happy" has declined over the same period of time in which the median family income has nearly doubled.

Robert Lane, a professor at Yale, argues that the leveling off and diminishment of happiness coinciding with rising income reflects the trade-off between the two sources of happiness—material comfort and social and familial intimacy. Modern economic development increases wealth by encouraging mobility, commercializing relationships, and giving us families in which all adults work. The result is greater income but weakened social and familial ties.

In less developed countries, the improvement in material benefit more than offsets the declines in social connectedness. At some point, however, the balance tips, and Lane believes this has occurred in the United States. He thinks that the United States will continue to become unhappier in the future as incomes rise. Lane cites as one basis for his argument the rise in clinical depression. He might also have mentioned addictions—both substance addictions (such as addictions to alcohol or other drugs) and process addictions (such as gambling addiction, relationship and sex addiction, and food addiction).

While depression, substance addictions, and process addictions all operate in different ways in the brain, each is a disease of isolation. Each is in part a reflection of an abnormal way in which the psyche has compensated for the lack of close, healthy familial and social relation-ships. What often makes the issue confusing is that these disorders often arise in the context of familial and social relations that seem very close, but because of their enmeshment and toxicity, these disorders produce an often stronger version of isolation than simply attenuated relationships.

If an individual does not experience happiness regularly during nor-mal times, he or she should start the healing process by completing an emotional inventory.

Here are some questions a person should ask himself or herself when beginning an emotional inventory:

1. *What is the quality of your thoughts?* There is just no getting around the powerful connection between what we think and what we experience. Negative thoughts tend to create nega-tive experiences. Depression and addiction thrive in an at-mosphere of negative thoughts. The difficulty, of course, is in how to change negative thinking. Thinking about the issue does not change negative thinking. Taking different actions and changing old patterns that underlie the negative beliefs are what can cause the quality of our thoughts to change.

2. *Do you try to control what you have no control over?* Depres-sion is often connected to a feeling of powerlessness. But often that feeling of being powerless derives from an emo-tional need to control what can't be controlled. We can't con-trol whether our sons or daughters are happy, or whether or not our law case is ultimately successful. This need to con-trol things that are beyond our control often reflects fears that tend to isolate us. These fears must be faced in order to take away their power in our lives.

3. *Do you understand what you can and can't control?* There are a lot of things we have no control over, but there are some things we do significantly impact. Some depressed people have the skewed impression that they have no control over anything. The truth is that we really do influence many things, such as where we work and the kind of job we have. A depressed lawyer may believe that he or she has no choice

but to work in a firm—even when he or she hates coming in to work each day. A good rule of thumb is that if we don't see more than two solutions to a problem, we are looking at it through a distorted lens.

4. *How good is your self-care?* Many of us learn to treat ourselves poorly. We eat a lousy breakfast, we don't get a full night's sleep, and we don't exercise. Over time, bad habits involving eating, sleeping, and/or exercising are almost guaranteed to cause major health problems.

5. *Do you nurture your spirit?* We make time for work and for sleep in our busy schedule, but what about taking time for learning, relationships, and solitude? Lawyers are in a profession that requires constant learning, but if learning in our profession does not stimulate us, we need to spend time learning in areas that do. Making time for relationships is just like watering tomatoes in the summer. If we don't learn to spend some time each day devoted to experiencing those relations that are important to us, then our vines will wither. Many studies show that individuals with active spiritual lives and practices—more secular practices such as yoga or meditation, or more religious ones such as regular church worship—will experience a significantly greater degree of happiness. The types of social relation networks that go with these activities also provide a guard against isolation in times of stress.

6. *Did you laugh today?* Many lawyers take themselves too seriously. Humor can help people connect. Over time, a lack of humor can become a sort of social dry rot.

7. *What did you look forward to today?* A good indication of an unlived life is one that seems to be trudging along on "autopilot." After a while, this can leave us feeling isolated as our emotions become more and more separate from what is actually happening in our lives. To be comfortable with ourselves, we must be present and aware and embrace the emotions we are feeling at any given moment. Once we are comfortable in our own skin, we can look forward to experiencing all the small moments that make up our lives, one day at a time.

8. *What do you look forward to tomorrow?* Just as injurious as having no hopes for the future is having unrealistic expectations. We can't enjoy life today if we are continually focused on the future. For example, we can't think that we will be happy *after* we finally settle the personal injury case that will push our practice over the hump. We must constantly re-evaluate our priorities to assure that they are not only reasonable, but enhance all aspects of our life.

9. *What do you do that makes you happy?* Some people answer this question with enthusiasm. Others are stumped. It is an important question. We must think seriously about the answer—it's what gives vitality, energy, and meaning to our life.

10. *With whom do you share your true self?* Lots of lawyers put so much effort into their lawyer persona that they lose a sense of who they really are. Gradually and unconsciously identifying with a persona allows part of an individual to be repressed. Denying who we are, or parts of ourselves, often leads to depression, addiction, and problems with relationships.

Once we complete this inventory, the next and most important step is making a change. Many of us move along in life until something shakes us up—a heart attack occurs, we get arrested for drinking and driving, or depression becomes so severe that it brings us to the psychiatrist's office. We usually don't change without severe pain. It doesn't have to be that way. Small incremental changes can often bring great relief. Talking with a licensed therapist or counselor can help us understand and deal with our own resistance to change, even those changes we know we need to make for the better.

CHAPTER TWENTY-EIGHT

Toward a Theory of Time

Our Experience of Time As a Way to Understand Meaning in Life

> *Time is but the stream I go a-fishing in. I drink at it; but while*
> *I drink, I see the sandy bottom and detect how shallow it is.*
> *Its thin current slides away, but eternity remains.*
> —Henry David Thoreau, *Walden*

WHAT IS THE MEANING of our relationship with time and how does it affect our perception of happiness, joy, and peace? I often hear lawyers talk about feeling pushed by work and family obligations. They feel that they don't have enough time for life. When lawyers feel this stress to achieve, they often lose their sense of time. It is similar to being caught up in an enjoyable activity, such as playing basketball, fishing, or gardening—during these activities we often lose track of time. The most important key to good health in a time- and achievement-driven world may be to understand the barriers, distractions, and facades we build to modulate our experience of time.

The progress of technology in our culture has vastly increased our experience of time and our need to get "somewhere" quickly. The question is: How does the human psyche handle this acceleration? How do the press of time and the quickness of electronic communication—the feeling that we should have instantaneous response or gratification—affect us as humans?

I see several things happening in response to this time crunch. I see the breakdown of social relationships that take time to grow and mature. In the modern world, there is simply not enough time for face-to-face relationships. Twenty years ago, I remember talking to a friend who lived in New York City who told me that he saw his best friend, who also lived in New York City, only once or twice a year. Now I find that I see some of my good friends only once or twice a year. There has been an increase in technology-mediated relationships such as those between friends who e-mail each other but rarely see each other in person.

On the physical level, I see the increase of autoimmune and chronic diseases influenced by stress. And isn't stress simply one of the physical symptoms caused by the experience of a world moving too fast? I see an increase in highly structured belief systems and communities. In the chaos of speeded-up time, people seem to need a container in which to be held. A strong belief system is one of the best ways to contain the threat to the psyche of the chaos of accelerated time. But these rigid systems also cause problems. A psyche under siege easily loses its ability to grow, to change, and to adapt.

Look at entertainment as a primary cultural experience. Our American culture has moved from the experience of novels that would absorb us for hours or days, to movies that rely more on the speed and action of visual stimulation than the creation of real meaningful human drama, which takes time.

Do addictions increase as we try to deal with the phenomenon of accelerated time? Many individuals use drugs because they want to slow time down, to escape the constant grinding forward of the wheels of time. But alcohol and other drug use eventually moves the user toward more chaos. To be caught in the chaos of addiction is the ultimate slavery, a complete loss of time.

As Carl Jung noted many years ago, the desire for alcoholic spirits may be the literal manifestation of spiritual desire. And just as some individuals use alcohol to achieve a feeling of slowing time down, many spiritual practices in the world's great religions also allow humans to come to grips with time. The practices of prayer and meditation are disciplines to put us in sync with the time flow of our inner self and to a connection to something larger than the self. Ironically, the urge to live in a state of spirituality often springs from the same desire as the urge to use drugs—the desire to slow down the relentless time-driven hoofbeat of reality. From the spiritual perspective, when time is slowed, life becomes much richer, more palpable and enjoyable—its energy flows freer.

Current psychological literature talks about humans' ability to achieve a "flow" state where we can engage with the world in such an authentic way that time seems to stand still. Hours can seem like minutes, and minutes stretch into hours. This way of being is synonymous with creativity.

There is a story of a white explorer who goes to Africa. He hires three native Africans to help him carry his equipment. They load up his gear and race forward for three days. At the end of the third day, the Africans sit down and will not move. The explorer urges them to get up and resume the journey, explaining the pressure he is under to reach his intended area of exploration by a certain date. They refuse to move. He continues to try to persuade them, but they will not move. Finally, one of the natives tells the explorer, "We have moved too quickly to reach this place. Now we need to give our spirits a chance to catch up with us."

Some alcoholics and other drug addicts have self-medicated themselves with these substances in an attempt to slow down a world that is too fast, that bombards their senses too aggressively. Others have abused substances because the world is moving too slowly for them, and boredom, the father of discovery of the self, has emerged. For many of us, self-discovery threatens to reveal our fears. We may use alcohol and other drugs to provide a buffer to help us avoid confronting these fears. Either way, the addiction experience blocks the natural rhythm of time.

One way to look at addiction is to see it as a disease that takes away the addict's conscious choice and experience of time. AA has found universal spiritual principles that allow each individual to come up with his or her unique solution to deal with the charge of time into the twenty-first century. For addicts broken apart by struggling to control the pace of time, there has been one approach, developed by the founders of AA, which is proven to work. This Twelve Step approach, grounded in the universal principles of spirituality, provides the tools that allow us to slow down the experience of time and to confront and discard the fears of the past. Perhaps the most famous slogan of AA is "One day at a time." For those who use the tools of AA to guide their lives, first things are handled first. Time becomes more manageable. Yet AA never suggests inflexible solutions; it gives creativity time to blossom.

CHAPTER TWENTY-NINE

Accommodation or Transformation

How Our Perspective on Life Can Be Transformed

THE HEART is the literal and metaphorical center of our lives. We may have an open heart (an open perspective toward life) or be "closed-hearted." Our response to life may be one full of heartache or heartfelt joy.

All of us have issues and challenges from time to time. How we respond will tell us something about how we feel in our heart, and how we respond will determine our emotional health. Issues that center around the heart and feelings are usually issues of transformation. Those issues not felt deeply are usually issues of accommodation. Often problems occur when transformation is needed but we settle for accommodation.

If I break my leg, I can go to the doctor and get the bone set and cast. I can use crutches and accommodate my schedule. Over time, my leg will heal and my heart will probably not be stressed at all in the process. But when we are faced with longer-term issues in our lives—chronic illnesses or disorders such as diabetes, alcoholism, attention deficit disorder, or depression—the challenge is different. We no longer have the option of accommodating to a short-term inconvenience, but we must come to terms with living a life with a disorder we did not anticipate or want. Often this is only possible through a transformation that involves a change of heart about how we see our life.

In talking with lawyers facing difficulties or particular times of stress, I am surprised to learn that they often say that their desire to become a lawyer in the first place came from some early injustice experienced in their life. These individuals might have grown up with a raging and abusive father. Or they may have grown up "dirt poor" and felt the harshness of struggling to survive and to succeed. These lawyers are driven by their desire to help make the world more just and fair for others. These early experiences, which were wounding, launched them into their career as a lawyer. In a sense, the wound is also a gift. It has given them a sense of determination and a keen sense of what is right and wrong and has propelled them forward.

However, most lawyers will at some point have to face up to the negative part of this wound—the part that makes them driven, that makes them feel overly responsible for seeing that justice is achieved. There must be a change of heart in which they come to terms with the past and see, often for the first time, the gift that came with the wound. In doing this, they open their hearts to themselves as well as to the clients they try to serve. Otherwise, they are apt to lapse into depression or addiction or become workaholics (or some combination of these) as a way to avoid dealing with the underlying feelings of unfairness and abuse. These individuals may be aggressive, hard-fighting lawyers on the exterior, but inside they are stuck in the identity of being a victim.

I remember one time reading a book on creativity. The author had researched people in many fields of endeavor—musicians, artists, bankers, and lawyers. All of the most creative individuals, regardless of their vocation, had one characteristic in common. They all accepted the reality of who they were and their external environment exactly the way it was. Their acceptance of themselves meant that all their energy went into their own creative passion. There was no lost effort in trying to make the world different from the way it actually was. Acceptance seems to be one of the characteristics of being open-hearted—acceptance of ourselves regardless of whether we have a chronic condition such as diabetes, alcoholism, attention deficit disorder, or depression. Such disorders can either be the starting place for acceptance or an enduring place of struggle that can go on endlessly.

As lawyers, we face the daily choice of accommodation or transformation in how we adapt to the technologies of cell phones, e-mails, and computers that all accelerate our lives. Are we accepting them as useful tools, or are these technologies running our lives? If they are running our lives, the chances are good that we are not allowed the chance to emotionally absorb our life and enjoy our daily activities.

Many lawyers who suffer from alcoholism or other drug addictions are also depressed. Often depression comes from difficulty in adjusting to the loss of the idealized view of how his or her life as a lawyer would actually be. Accepting the reality of the world of law requires an emotional adjustment that takes time and an open attitude. Too often lawyers avoid challenging feelings by simply working long hours. What starts off as simple emotional avoidance can, over time, become a pattern that leads to the onset of clinical depression.

Individuals with a chronic disease, such as alcoholism or depression, often seek a solution of accommodation rather than transformation. An alcoholic must remain abstinent and learn to handle his or her mood without drinking. The depressed individual must let go of his or her fear and examine any unresolved emotional issues. The diabetic must come to terms with the need for ongoing medication and diet control.

For almost all of these chronic problems, good nutrition, exercise, and medication may all be part of the solution. However, any one factor alone may simply be an accommodation to the problem when what is needed is personal transformation. In the case of lawyers, this involves a willingness to be openhearted toward himself or herself and a reordering of priorities and self-acceptance that brings meaning to life by giving the "self" back to the world.

CHAPTER THIRTY

Against the Pollution of the "I"

How Our Inner Vision Shapes What We See
As the Outer World

JACQUES LUSSEYRAN was born in 1924. At school one day when he was eight, as classes ended and he was rushing for the door, he was accidentally shoved. He fell, hitting his head on one of the sharp corners of the teacher's desk. He was wearing glasses and the blow drove one of the arms of his glasses deep into his right eye. He lost consciousness. When he came to, he was permanently blind in both eyes.

Later he was to write that barely ten days after the accident he made a discovery that continued to entrance him for the rest of his life. He found that if, rather than looking out, he looked inward, he could see. As he described it, his experience of seeing was real and concrete. There was a light that he experienced coming from within, and that light illuminated what was around him.

A second great discovery soon followed. There was only one way Lusseyran could turn on the inner light. If he was overwhelmed with feelings of resentment or sorrow, then the light faded. If he experienced joy and love, the light increased. He stated this "discovery was so great that a whole lifetime full of religion and morality is often not enough to enable others to make it." Yet he made that discovery as an eight-year-old child.

What a thought to ponder. What would it mean in our lives if we had to love in order to see? Certainly Lusseyran experienced uncomfortable emotions such as anger or sadness. But in order to see, he could not let himself be attached to such emotions. Resentment is attachment to anger. In order to see, Lusseyran had to let go of his negative emotions and be open to the joy of life.

The poet Robert Bly once said that our greatest wound is the source of our greatest gift. Lusseyran found that because of his blindness he had to develop a forgotten faculty, the faculty of attention. He became more attentive to himself, to others, and to the world around him. Through the development of the power of attention, we develop the capacity for being completely present. Lusseyran found that by being completely present he was open to the joy of life, open to a very physical experience of the animating force in all things. By tuning in to that and being very attentive, Lusseyran found that he would not run into objects; by being attentive he could discern whether he was walking under maples or oaks.

Lusseyran discovered that every object and living thing revealed itself to him as a kind of quiet yet unmistakable pressure that indicates its intention and form. What he described is like the magnified experience of realizing suddenly that someone has walked into the room and is standing behind you. You have not heard the person, but you sense his or her presence. For Lusseyran, this sensitivity to the presence of things became his way of being in the world.

Shortly after he graduated from high school, Lusseyran's native France was invaded by the Nazis, and within five weeks Paris was occupied. He said that he experienced the invasion by the Nazis as a second blindness—the experience of the loss of freedom in the external world was like his experience of being blinded. After being in shock for a few weeks, he reacted as he had to his first blindness, by looking internally for freedom. With the clarity of his internal vision, he entered the underground French resistance movement. Because of his inner sight, he became the person who determined who could be allowed to enter the resistance group he organized, which wrote and published an underground newspaper. He became the blind leader of six hundred sighted comrades.

In July 1943, the Gestapo arrested Lusseyran. He was interrogated for forty-five days, kept in jail for six months, and in January 1944 was taken to the Buchenwald concentration camp. Of the two thousand French nationals who arrived in Buchenwald the day Lusseyran did, only thirty were alive when the United States Third Army liberated the camp.

Lusseyran survived, he believed, for two reasons: because in the worst of moments, he could always turn inward to a source of help, and because he found a way to be useful to his community of prisoners. He served his fellow prisoners by speaking several languages and setting up a system of prisoner communications. He could turn inward not because he simply had faith, but because his blindness had given him an experience of the reality of his faith. He said, "Every time the sight and the tests of the camp became unbearable, I closed myself off from the world. I entered a refuge where the SS could not reach me. I directed my gaze toward that inner light which I had seen when I was eight years old. I let it swing through me. And quickly I made the discovery that the light was life—that it was love. Now I could again open my eyes—and also my ears and nose—to the slaughter and the misery. I survived them."

What Lusseyran experienced was the all-important truth that our fate is shaped from within ourselves and emanates outward into our lives as actualized on the physical plane. Lusseyran said that one of the most powerful lessons of his blindness was in coming to understand the illusion of believing that life is about progressing from one form to another. He came to know that if we believe that what we see externally encompasses reality then we become a sort of idolater. For Lusseyran, seeing was interplay of internal and external worlds. In blindness, he learned that freedom is internal, personal, and subjective, but at the same time mutually dependent on interaction with the rest of creation.

Lusseyran also made a discovery about impatience. He said, "When I was impatient, I wanted everything to go faster. I wanted to eat quickly. And during this time, all the objects immediately started to turn against me like fretful children." Impatience, he found, is a form of arrogance. It affected his inner/outer seeing like resentment or anger. The antidote to impatience was joy. Joy is captured by being a part of the world on the world's terms. Impatience only drives further away the thing that we are impatient for. It is, he suggests, impossible to be happy and impatient at the same time. If he could not hold joy inside, he could not see.

One of the most intriguing essays written by Lusseyran is called "Against the Pollution of the I." He distinguishes the "I" he is talking about from the ego, which he calls the outer manifestation of the "I."

The ego is the part that reads self-help books, that thinks it can fix itself, that lives in the extremes of grandiosity—either as the controlling person who must dominate to feel okay or the victim who must stay in self-pity. The ego needs things. The "I" makes no such demands.

Lusseyran argued in his essay that our sacred inner space—in which, though blinded, he found his ability to see—is being taken over by a barrage of external stimuli from the flashing images of the modern world on radio, television, and the cinema. Lusseyran died before computers and the Internet became a part of the bombardment of the psyche by the external world. But he would have certainly included them. Lusseyran's concern was—to use the information-age analogy—that the operating program of the person has been corrupted by a virus so that rather than giving clear images from the "I," what is received is distorted, lacking in any personal truth. Lusseyran believed that the "I" only learns through experience and that it nourishes itself exclusively on its own activity. He feared the pollution of the "I" was leading to the death of the "I" for many people. Lusseyran sees the loss of the "I" in the work of famous postmodern writers and artists who wish to deconstruct everything, to create metaphysics of absences. When the "I" dies, the person loses the ability to see, the ability to survive concentration camps, the ability to be attentive, the ability to know and feel the world external to the "I"—the ability to love.

The greatest pollution of the "I" seen by Lusseyran was in alcohol and other drug use. We drink alcohol because it works; it allows us to change our mood and the way we feel. We drink to avoid the "I." Young people go to rock concerts to get "high" in order to eliminate their "I-ness." Individuals take cocaine to feel happy. Lusseyran noted, "Owning an 'I' is not easy, and keeping it is even harder. Perhaps the search for happiness is not the right approach." Further, Lusseyran said, "I understand very well why so many young people are drawn to drugs. I understand, you may be sure, that they want to draw a curtain over a world in which entire populations or huge forests are wiped out every day, where persecution is not a matter of passion but of calculated science . . . I well understand that they are possessed of only one desire: to get away. But if they leave, do they ever arrive? They really ought to be told that they never will arrive!"

You never arrive, Lusseyran believed, because the "I" is left behind.

Drugs work against the "I" and set upon it to ravage it. They live through its absence . . . As human beings, we have all been touched by the force that we call "the I," but it is not riveted to our bodies. It is at all times ready to give up its place. It practically cries out for its own submergence by things, by numbers, by systems, by endless pleasure, and by drugs. And that is why I say that there is danger, most pressing danger. The "I" is being polluted even more rapidly than the earth.

CHAPTER THIRTY-ONE

Reconnecting through Experience

How the Process of Emotional Healing Works

WHAT IS THE NATURE of emotional healing? How do we regain a sense of centeredness or wholeness? In the tradition of the Tao, there is a saying: "The Way that can be spoken about is not the Way." Or in other words, those who know the answers to these questions don't speak them, and those that don't know, talk on and on. This warning suggests that if we think that obtaining wholeness and serenity in our lives is something simply to be learned intellectually, we will inevitably be disappointed. This is a particularly good warning for lawyers. We want to understand intellectually, because in intellectual understanding there is the illusion of control.

Fortunately or unfortunately, the door to healing opens not through the intellect, but through experience and the emotional nature of experience. To only try the door of the intellect is to try to control experience, which inevitably erects a barrier between the direct knowledge of what the experience is about. Not that the intellect isn't important in finding a door—it is. But the intellect is simply not the way we enter. Therefore, I, as an author, am presumptively off on the wrong foot by trying to write about a process that must be experienced directly, rather than by the intellectual process of reading about it. But despite this difficulty, maybe it is still possible to talk in a way that will be helpful, not necessarily to entering the door to recover centeredness, but at least to finding that door.

Let me start with a metaphorical description of what must be overcome to regain our center and heal our emotions. I am not trying to describe the way a particular school of psychology sees things, but a way to generally understand several different psychological points of view.

Let's start with the process by which addiction and depression occur, whether caused by growing up in an alcoholic home, by the fragmentation of time, or by some capricious trauma. In response to trauma, our centeredness breaks in some way. If we look at the psyche as comprising a person's mental, physical, emotional, and spiritual aspects, then when trauma occurs, the mainline defense of the psyche is to split off— to disassociate so the impact of the trauma will be reduced and the person is not overwhelmed. This split can happen with one single event or as part of a gradual process over time.

When we disassociate ourselves from our psyche, we often seek ways to lessen the psychic tension of the split. It is not the event itself that our psyche tries to fix but the emotional consequences of the tearing event. There are several key dysfunctional choices. Usually we "choose" one or more of these dysfunctional paths in the portion of the psyche that is split off. If, for example, a female child is sexually abused, she may disassociate from her physical body. If a male child is taught that emotions are bad, he may disassociate from his emotional aspect. If a child is religiously abused, he or she may disassociate from his or her spiritual aspect.

There are several key ways that the disassociation is perpetuated, but addiction is a primary one. The use of alcohol or other drugs to alter mood creates the illusion of control by meeting the need caused by the disassociation. For example, the abused child will crave relief from the pain of the splitting psychic injury. As an adult, this individual may self-medicate against the pain with alcohol or other drugs. Repeated use of drugs to relieve pain can set up a physiological craving in which the brain receives a strong, constant message: He or she cannot live without the chemical. When this happens, addiction has set in. Alcoholism and other addictions may not always result from a psychic injury, but often they do.

On a psychological level something similar happens with process addictions. A process addiction may be an addiction to a relationship, sex, gambling, shopping, or working. In the case of a process addiction, the chemical setting up the addictive chain reaction is not coming from outside the body, but is being generated in the brain itself.

Whether it is an external or internal chemical, the process in the addictive cycle is similar though the physiology is very different. The individual medicates to alter his or her mood, then has a momentary feeling of relief, then feels worse after drinking too much, working too much, or spending too much. Feeling guilty about the behavior leads to more use, which continues the addictive cycle.

Another way that addicted people try to cope with a disassociation of the psyche is through the illusion of control. A person may feel that if he or she can control or significantly influence events, then everything will be okay. Of course, like addiction, control as a means to avoid angst is also fated not to work, because one can never really control life. Underneath the need to control is fear. Control often centers on issues of unconscious anxiety about not having enough. If there is enough money, enough security, or enough power, for example, then the individual believes he or she will be insulated from the fear and insecurity that goes with a split psyche. However, for this individual, enough can never truly be enough. There is always the fear that what he or she has will not *be* enough.

The emergence of different schools of psychology over the past one hundred years is in part due to different practitioners focusing on different ways the psyche reacts to psychic splits. Freud and his followers exposed the empty cycle of the insatiable longing for oral and sexual gratification to feel okay. Humanistic psychology emphasized human potential. Ego psychology, behaviorism, and cognitive therapy have focused on ways to strengthen the ego structure that has been injured. Each separate theory has sought to reclaim a missing piece of the human psyche.

Perhaps a broader perspective comes from Buddhist psychology, which sees issues of addiction, power and control, and security as all part of our fear of experiencing ourselves directly. In Buddhist terms, the various types of suffering that make up life illuminate the core question of "Who am I?" In Buddhism, suffering is the problem, but it is also the solution. Or put in Western terms, as long as we are driven by addiction or neurosis, we will never get to know ourselves, but it is the nature of those very things that split us off from ourselves that also offer the opportunity to reveal who we are. Said another way, the causes of suffering are also the means of release; it is the individual's perspective that determines whether he or she is enslaved by trauma or whether it becomes a passage to maturity, self-knowledge, and fulfillment. You may have heard the expression "thinking controls experience." If our experience is poor, all we need to do is change our thinking or perspective.

For most of us, the starting place to healing is to redevelop our own spirituality as a way of being. Those who developed AA and the Twelve Step method of recovery understood that we cannot begin to recover a normal emotional life without first reacquiring a spiritual connection. A spiritual connection provides a support outside of the psyche so that the things in chaos in the psyche can be repaired.

By "spiritual" I don't mean "religious," although this may well be. Individuals working the Twelve Steps often say that religion is for those afraid of hell and that spirituality is for those who have been there. This is an oversimplification, but we get the point. A spiritual connection is made by experience, not by intellect. The ways to do this are so simple that we tend to overlook them in our time-driven lives. Experiencing such connections takes time. Spiritual connection might come from communing with nature or reading inspired literature, or it might come from the support of a group of like-minded people trying to overcome a fatal disease, but it is the experience that allows the psyche to have faith in something outside of itself that begins to set the stage for healing to begin.

People in Twelve Step programs have discovered that this connection is not something that we have to believe in for it to occur. Rather we have to be simply willing to believe that it is possible. We must be open to the possibility of new experience. In fact, the very nature of spirituality is to open and free the psyche from rigidities and inflexibilities that have arisen to try to stay the feelings of disease. Once there is spiritual connection, it is possible to experience the nature of the wounds in the psyche differently and for a shift in our view of experience to occur.

Often, once the spirituality connection is made and fostered, the work in later recovery becomes to regain the emotional aspect that has been cut off. This requires that we learn how to feel without being numb or overwhelmed with feelings. It also might mean that we need to regain the physical aspect that has been disassociated—to become centered in and grounded in our body without being numb to it. In either case, the process of later recovery often involves learning a certain amount of detachment.

I had a fear of the idea of detachment. It conjured up in my mind the idea of being removed from life. Detachment, as it is used in the Buddhist tradition and Twelve Step work, is a way to open—to take in the fullness of life. Many addicts report that the volume of the world just seems to be turned up too high. They may feel the need to self-medicate as a way to turn down the excessive stimulation. In our fast-paced world, we can get caught in a cycle of feeling stressed by hyperstimulation, but then feeling empty when we are not being driven. Detachment can offer a way to modulate sensory input so it is neither underwhelming nor overwhelming.

Learning detachment is an experiential process, not an intellectual one. It comes after people reconnect to their spiritual life. If it is made before or without spiritual connection, it is a dry, ego-centered process that may calm, but not heal. If made after or in conjunction with the re-emergence of spiritual connection, the entire personality is vivified. Ultimately, the process of opening through detachment leads to a shift from a spatially based experience of life as outside the self, to a temporal experience of life in which we are not separate from the experience. In this state, we can experience life not as something external rushing by, but with the inner self as a part of the ongoing flow of life itself.

CHAPTER THIRTY-TWO

Experience the Present

Learning to Let Go of Regret about the Past and Fear of the Future

MANY BUSY INDIVIDUALS, including lawyers, live life trying to get through the day so they can check one more thing off their lists. Is life, in fact, just a series of tasks? Are we just waiting to complete some unseen list, so life can begin?

We are well trained to live in the future. I remember when my son was a junior in high school and couldn't wait to graduate so he could go to college. I remember when I couldn't wait to get out of college, and then I couldn't wait to get out of law school. At a meeting today, I heard one lawyer say that for the next three months he had no time for anything but work. The truth is that we can't live in the future; we can only occupy the present. Life is what happens while we are getting ready for it to begin.

Living in the past is just as bad as living for the future. There are several ways we live in the past. One is by attachment to regret, blame, and loss. We make mistakes, and we miss opportunities. And most of all, we have losses. If we do not deal with these normal but difficult life events, they can alter how we experience life. If we do not grieve our losses, the present is always colored by what *happened.* If we do not make matters right with the people we have harmed, then we are never really able to enjoy a full relationship with them (and perhaps others like them) again.

Another way we live in the past is captured in the expression "You never get enough of what you don't want." Or "If you keep on doing the same thing, you will keep on getting the same results." We may live in the past by acting out of old ways of being that are no longer applicable to our present reality. For example, if an individual grows up in an alcoholic household, he or she may learn that surviving requires developing acute senses for avoiding an alcoholic parent's rages or changing moods. After a while, this survival skill becomes a script for becoming dependent on the moods of others, such as a spouse or friend. It is not a good script for having wholesome adult relations, especially intimate ones, but if not examined and understood it can continue to run this individual's life.

Living in the past or the future both revolve around trying to alter our emotional state in the present—an inability to accept the circumstances of our lives that are beyond our control. Lawyers often have difficulty experiencing their present emotional state. Why? We often like to be in control. Emotions seem chaotic, and if we are not used to fully feeling our emotions, then to experience them is to feel out of control. A lawyer's choice of profession may reflect a need for order and certainty. We come to our vocation with a natural inclination away from our emotional aspect. Our emotional being is like a pair of shoes. Until they are "broken in," the experience of our emotions is going to seem, at best, uncomfortable and, at worst, possibly downright scary.

As lawyers, many of us come to legal careers with a natural tendency to shy away from our emotional aspect, to have emotional shoes that have never been broken in. Then, when we experience a significant emotional event—the death of a loved one, the loss of a job, a divorce, or even the loss of a major case—the response of the psyche is to want to close down or avoid, rather than encounter, this significant emotional experience. As lawyers we may find ourselves ill equipped for the normal emotional challenges of life.

True enjoyment of life is an emotional experience. At any time we can learn not to be an observer of life but an emotional participant in it. We can fantasize or intellectualize about what we would like the future to be, but we can only truly be in the present emotionally. For many of us, the impetus to change our way of being—to quit living in the future or quit being stuck in the past—will only come through some significant emotional crisis of loss.

Loss is with us every day. Every time we gain something, we also give up something. Even the loss of something we view as negative, like a bad marriage, is also an occasion of real grief. Not only do we lose people from our lives, we also suffer the loss of dreams, plans, and ideas. In our fast-paced, technology-driven society, we have less and less time to experience our losses, to gain understanding from the experience, and to grow into new ways of living that build on what we learned from our losses. Our emotional clock runs on a more tribal, primitive time that is not linear. Loss is not something to be fixed. Emotional experience teaches us the things that can't be learned from books: compassion, gratitude, and what it is like to stand in someone else's shoes—in essence, what it means to be a human being.

The effective handling of emotions always involves other people. In order to be secure experiencing feelings of loss, we need to trust another person with whom we can share our losses. The kind of person we need is someone who is not going to try to fix it, rationalize why it might be good, or minimize the loss, but who can simply be with us and allow us to experience our grief. As we "break in" our own emotional shoes, we will become the kind of person who can fully experience feelings of loss and can be a supportive listener for someone we care about.

Participating in social rituals that acknowledge our losses also help us effectively handle these challenging emotions. Wakes and funerals are rituals that allow us to take action with others to memorialize loss, and the meaning that was present which the loss has taken away. These are very important ways for the psyche to absorb loss in a healthy way. Of course, most of us recognize the negative emotional extremes—lawyers who run their careers on anger because of their own unaddressed emotional issues. Or those who still can't get out of bed two years after the death of a loved one. In fact, it is our fear of the extremes that often pushes us away from breaking in our emotional shoes. But the emotional extremes are usually reflections of defective emotional growth, and not ways of being that are likely to be encountered by individuals who accept their emotional nature.

How do we know when we have not really come to terms with loss? Loss affects us emotionally, physically, intellectually, and spiritually. Loss—particularly loss that is not actively grieved—can result in stress that decreases the functioning of the immune system. Other physical symptoms of loss, particularly unprocessed loss, may include nausea, headaches, and chronic tiredness. Addiction to nicotine, food, gambling, and sex can all be triggered by the stress caused by loss, particularly where there is a family history of addictive illness.

Emotional responses to loss include anger, sadness, fear, and guilt. These responses may be appropriate. However, if the loss is not grieved, such emotional responses can become stuck, much like a needle caught on a record, and play over and over, causing harmful physical consequences such as those described in the previous paragraph.

Particularly in the early stages of significant loss, it is possible to experience significant problems in cognitive functioning—including confusion, disorientation, difficulty concentrating, and memory problems. Since the intellectual arena is usually a lawyer's strong suit, this sort of experience from loss often feels very destabilizing.

Finally, loss may be a real spiritual challenge. It can start us on the road to questioning the meaning of life, particularly when the loss is out of natural sequence, as when a child dies before a parent. Loss can cause life to seem meaningless or, through the process of grieving, loss may allow a spiritual connection to be regained or allow us to find a spiritual life that never existed before. Despite all the horrible things that happen in the world and humankind's ongoing inhumanity to itself, the world is a pretty wondrous place to be. This is a realization that is comprehended emotionally, never just with the rational mind.

So where do you start if you spend most of your time living in the future or the past? Begin to break in your emotional shoes. As with learning any new skill, such as playing tennis or using a new computer program, it helps to have a teacher. This kind of teacher is called a therapist. If you have an addiction in your life, the process of successful recovery is most often directed through the use of the Twelve Steps. Working the Steps will help you learn how to be comfortable—without drugs, food, sex, or whatever the addiction is—in your own emotional shoes. Start by finding a Twelve Step group where you belong, and find a therapist or someone else you can talk to authentically on a regular basis about how you feel.

Try on a new mantra, such as "Time is my ally," or the Zen koan "Without doing anything, let nothing be undone." The passage of time is one of the most present realities in all our lives. Time is not what we are waiting for—time is what's happening right now. Once you have broken in your emotional shoes, the course correction that is often needed may be just a few degrees, not a ninety-degree turn. Focus on making the small changes in your life that make you more emotionally free to be who you are each day, each hour, each minute of your life. These kinds of changes make time your friend.

ut of the Box

Shifting How One Experiences Life

A LAWYER NAMED DANIEL recently told me about attending a retreat where he heard the words "Life does not have to be a burden." He said these simple words changed many things in his life, even years after he first heard them. Before the retreat, Daniel's experience in practicing law, being a husband, and being a father were all from the perspective of feeling weighed down by life. It wasn't that he never had fun or didn't enjoy what he was doing with his life. Instead, it was simply that life often seemed like an obligation, a chore, an endless list of the things he had to do. He thought that this was the perspective from which most people lived their lives. He had stopped enjoying practicing law. Work had become a never-ending process of client phone calls to return, appointments to be kept, and deadlines to be met.

Daniel was lucky. He had the opportunity for insight into his own experience of life before depression, anxiety disorders, and addiction became the defense of the psyche against feeling its own deadness. His perspective changed just a few degrees. He realized he did not have to control so tightly or demand so much of himself and others, and that his life could become joyous and fulfilling. What allowed Daniel to experience a shift in perspective of how he experienced life?

To understand how Daniel's experience of his life changed, let's take a look at how the psyche or the human spirit grows. When we are young, we all have heroes. Sometimes they are professional athletes. Somehow these heroes exhibit a skill, ability, and a spirited way of living life that we admire. Our psyche grows by projection. We sense traits we admire in other people, and we are drawn to them as a way to understand and develop those same traits in ourselves. We grow up by wanting to be like something greater than ourselves. Because something out-side of us has greater meaning, we are pulled forward to develop as human beings.

While we need to internalize characteristics, such as honesty and in-tegrity, of those we admire, we never outgrow the need for something outside of ourselves to continue to pull us forward in our growth as individuals. In the 1930s, Bill Wilson, one of the cofounders of AA, stumbled onto the awkward phrase of "Higher Power." Despite the awkwardness of the term, it reflects Wilson's recognition that human growth only occurs by connection to or seeking connection with some-thing greater than the self. The application of this principle in AA has been so profound that it has allowed millions of men and women af-flicted with the chronic disease of addiction to have fulfilling and re-warding lives.

Daniel had come up against the wall of a life self-contained. He had a good law practice, a nice house and family, but no connection with some meaning greater than himself to pull his life forward. This con-nection to something greater is what is often called spirituality. I don't mean this in a religious or esoteric sense—rather, in the sense of a young child who runs free playing across the lawn and whose connec-tion with life might be described by his or her grandmother as being that of a "spirited child." It is that lived sense of joy and freedom that was missing in Daniel's life.

Too often, I run into lawyers who are living in the anteroom of de-pression or addiction. These diseases are biological, psychological, and spiritual. Their impact can force us to wrestle with what life means. These lawyers are smart, desire to do good work, and have great talent, but are living a life that has become a burden. There is nothing outside of them pulling them forward into their greatest potential as human be-ings. Sometimes a cause will pull a lawyer along for a while, but if com-mitment is based only on ego, eventually the lawyer will suffer from burnout.

Getting "outside the box" is somehow connected with living a more heartfelt life. There are several different traditional approaches to open-ing the heart and getting out of this box. In the East, Buddhism has over the centuries developed an abstract idea of what a Higher Power is. This abstract notion is balanced in the East by practices such as meditation, which are designed to open the heart. In the West, the more traditional idea of a Higher Power usually takes one of two forms. Traditional religious practices suggest the idea of devotion and personal relationship to an object of worship, which opens the heart. Another traditional route of devotional practice is seen in those who care particularly about the natural world, gardens, and wilderness. Working in the humus can be devotional. The root of the words "humus" and "humility" is the same. People with open hearts are humble, open-minded, and refuse to live based on stereotypes.

Part of Bill Wilson's genius was to recognize not only the importance of a Higher Power, but that everyone needs the freedom to work out what that means for himself or herself. An addicted person may have to lose family, fortune, and career before deciding that he or she needs help from something outside himself or herself. The answer to moving beyond a stuck place in life is to find some greater purpose outside ourselves that will pull us forward. If you are feeling that your life is just a burden, there is a way for you to connect within yourself and get out of the box. Start by talking about meaning in your life with someone you trust.

CHAPTER THIRTY-FOUR

Reap the Promises

How Changing Our Experience of Life
Changes Our Life

One morning I went to a place beyond dawn.
A source of sweetness that flows and is never less.
I have been shown a beauty that would confuse both worlds,
but I won't cause that uproar.

—Rumi

NO MATTER HOW WE GROW UP—wealthy or poor, well loved or forsaken—we form a view of life. Everything we do is based on the belief that our view of life is how things truly are. Many lawyers have had the experience of standing before a judge who, after hearing only two or three minutes of a case (say it's a slip-and-fall case), appears to have a preconceived notion that he or she knows what the case is really about (maybe the customer was negligent in some way). We know intuitively as lawyers that we have our work cut out for us, and that the rest of the trial will be about trying to convince the judge that this case is different from what he or she believes.

Why should we protest when a judge does this to us, when this is what we do to ourselves over and over again? We unconsciously sort our experiences into pre-existing categories based on how we think the world is. What happens when we run into events that call into question our view of life? For example, if you grew up in an environment in which you easily learned to trust that others would not hurt you but later encounter a situation in which someone is intent on doing you harm, you may react foolishly because this situation doesn't fit with your beliefs about how people are. When we run into a situation that calls into question our view of life, we often react by either ignoring or closing down, or by trying to manipulate or control the situation to avoid bringing our view of life into question.

For those of us with addictive disease, addictive personalities, or high control needs, the tendency to avoid something that runs counter to our belief system is very high indeed. While this might not be a huge problem if we have a fairly wide-ranging belief system, one of the things alcoholism, other addictive diseases, and depression do is constrain and compress an individual's world view. Alcoholism and other addictive diseases are diseases of isolation, and with the avoidance of close personal relations comes a narrowing of how one sees the world—the world and other people become less trustworthy, more suspect.

All of this explains why many addicts may be, as yet, unable to comprehend the promises of AA. Particularly if an individual has a substance abuse problem, the promises of AA may be outside of his or her current belief system. Belief systems are based largely on the learning that occurs as a result of experience. Addiction brings with it an experience of guilt, remorse, and shame. The cumulative effect of continually experiencing these feelings is the loss of hope—hope that anything will ever be different. Without hope, we are not able to comprehend the radical promises of AA. People who participate in AA experience hope through attending meetings long before the promises become part of their belief systems.

The poet Rumi wrote about the promises in "both worlds" from the perspective of experiential understanding, cognitive meaning, and his own spiritual enlightenment. Perhaps foolishly, I offer the promises of AA here for two reasons. First, something so powerful that it has literally saved the lives of millions of people needs to be shared, even though those who most need these promises will reject them out of hand. Second, there is a universality to the promises that is profound. In *Essential Spirituality* by Roger Walsh, the author looks at the seven great world religions—Judaism, Christianity, Islam, Hinduism, Buddhism, Confucianism, and Taoism—and discerns that, while their belief systems are divergent, all seven religions have certain practices in common. I was struck by the similarity between the benefits of these practices and the promises that several hopeless alcoholics made after implementing the Twelve Steps in their lives. They found, as Walsh has found, that if certain steps are followed, certain gifts result. Walsh describes the benefits of these common spiritual practices as including the following:

- reduced negative emotions such as fear and anger
- greater openness in life
- less of a tendency to depression and worry
- greater forthrightness in life
- increased serenity and peace
- greater emotional openness to the world
- a feeling of inner completeness
- greater emotional flexibility in caring for others
- more experiences of lightness and joy
- a greater receptivity to the world and to others
- a curiosity about the world and about life

The promises of AA offer similar benefits as can be seen in this excerpt from *Alcoholics Anonymous,* also known as the Big Book, pages 83 to 84:

If we are painstaking about this phase of our development, we will be amazed before we are half way through. We are going to know a new freedom and a new happiness. We will not regret the past nor wish to shut the door on it. We will comprehend the word serenity and we will know peace. No matter how far down the scale we have gone, we will see how our experience can benefit others.

For those who live with or love a substance-impaired person, there is also hope in the promises of Al-Anon. The following is from *From Survival to Recovery,* page 269:

If we willingly surrender ourselves to the spiritual discipline of the Twelve Steps, our lives will be transformed. We will become mature, responsible individuals with a great capacity for joy, fulfillment, and wonder. Though we may never be perfect, continued spiritual progress will reveal to us our enormous potential. We will discover that we are both worthy of love and loving. We will love others without losing ourselves, and will learn to accept love in return. Our sight, once clouded and confused, will clear and we will be able to perceive reality and recognize truth. Courage and fellowship will replace fear.

The wonderful benefits of a Twelve Step recovery program are available to those who want them. Recovering people often speak of having a moment of clarity, when for a moment their old belief system did not hold them back and they realized that it was possible for them to want these gifts in their lives.

The gifts of the promises come as a part of the process of working the Steps, and one of the key lessons of the Steps is learning to be of service. In a healthy individual there are at least three stages one goes through in which service work is important to develop the personality. The first stage is the idealistic stage. It is important that young adults go through this stage. To develop a healthy value system, young people need to feel sufficiently strong about their ideas and values to act upon them. It is the experience of acting on their values that allows what is valued to have resonance in their personality. Service can be a way to experience personal values and grow from them in the same way one might grow from a painful emotional experience.

In the normal, healthy sequence of development, idealism as a motivation for service will become tempered. The person who first sees the issue as entirely black or white will begin to see the gray nuances. The values will still be there, but the person will be less judgmental about those values. Youthful idealism will no longer be the motivation to do service work.

The second stage is what might be called the "Rotary Club stage." In this stage, one is interested in service work in order to be a part of the larger community. There is a healthy component of self-interest here. Service organizations are a way to become known, to make contacts, and to help get things done. Much of the important work that is done on Bar committees is the result of second-stage service work. This is a valuable and significant stage for growth through participation in activities based upon meaningful values. These activities offer an opportunity to become a part of something larger than us.

The third stage of development is one that a person rarely gets to before midlife. At this stage, one does service work not to impress others or to feel that one belongs, but because of one's relation to one's self. The service given is because of who an individual is on the inside. In the third stage, a person is not acting out of an external value system that defines what is right, or a need for external approval, but out of his or her own character. This type of service work, the experience of activities selflessly undertaken, is what deepens and refines character. This is the stage in which the character work gets done that builds the personalities of people who we all admire such as Gandhi or Mother Teresa.

In the field of addiction treatment, a cognitive approach has little efficacy. Chemical addiction is in part a disease of the brain. People who think about not wanting to drink as a way to get better just become more and more obsessed with drinking. Treatment for alcoholism is not based on thinking your way out of the problem, but on taking action to experience a new pattern of living. In fact, for the normal, healthy adult, the process of emotional maturation is also primarily one of growth through action, through experience. For example, we don't think about what it is like to experience the death of a parent and grow emotionally by having thought about that experience, rather we get real emotional growth by living through the experience of the parent's death.

One of the greatest attributes of AA is that its founders recognized the connection between service work and the rebuilding of a mature and healthy personality structure. The prescription for the self-centeredness caused by chemical addiction's narrowing of the personality's focus onto alcohol or another drug is to learn to be of service. It is the way in which the character eroded by disease-driven behavior is restored. Working with individuals of strong character is one of the reasons I enjoy working with volunteers who are in recovery. In short, most of these lawyers have been faced with the potentially fatal illness of addiction, and in the process of accepting what is necessary to cope with their illness, they also get sent to "advanced character school." Persons trying to heal don't know this is going to happen. In the beginning they are simply at their wits' end about how to deal with the chaos in their life caused by chemical addiction. Character building is a byproduct of those who seriously commit to work the Twelve Steps of AA. This character building comes through selfless service.

Most of us enjoy the feeling of being of service, but the truth is that we would like to get credit for it. Selfless service does not come easily. Here is a challenge for those ready for third stage character work: Do one act of service anonymously each day. It doesn't have to be big. It might be getting to work early and making coffee for everyone else. Like a lot of little things that make a big difference, this sounds easy or small. The experience of doing is what counts. We are fortunate to have a number of lawyers in our Bar who have, in their own individual ways, walked this walk. Not only do we admire these lawyers for their selfless service, but we also recognize them as individuals for whom the promises of recovery have come true.

CHAPTER THIRTY-FIVE

Learn to Reconnect

Healing through the Process of Connection

NO MATTER WHAT the ultimate problem—be it depression, narcissistic personality disorder, a substance addiction, or a process addiction—the incubator for most mental health issues is the family system. Family dysfunction is passed from generation to generation; often a generation has no idea what normal is. The seedbed of family problems is characterized by four norms:

- Isolation—the tendency to disconnect whenever something is emotionally uncomfortable
- Inhumanity—the widespread prevalence of emotional, physical, and sexual abuse
- Inconsistency—the lack of predictable behavior from parent figures
- Indoctrination—being told nothing is wrong when something clearly is (the mixed message)

A child's response to family behavior that isolates the child is not to talk, to family inhumanity is not to feel, to family inconsistency is not to trust, and to indoctrination is not to think. Healing cannot occur until the problem is understood—until we can get beyond being a victim and recognize how the very survival skills we adapted in childhood betray us as an adult.

The North Carolina Mecklenburg County Bar, following a string of eight suicides in just about that many years, established a Lawyer Support Committee consisting of professional clinicians and trained lawyer peer counselors as a means to reach out to and provide support to lawyers in that local Bar who needed help. This was the first such outreach of its kind in North Carolina, and remains a model for any local Bar whose members wish to help take responsibility for addressing lawyers who need help and believe they have nowhere to turn. Despite the availability of other community resources, lawyers are ultimately more willing to seek help from fellow lawyers. We respond to this kind of connection.

It is almost impossible to get people to agree on a definition of spirituality or mental health, but most people can define what these are not. Spirituality is not:

- judgmental
- material
- self-centered
- vain
- intolerant
- fear inducing
- physical
- ritualistic
- dogmatic
- time constrained
- magic
- guilt provoking
- anger engendering
- compulsive
- limited
- chaotic
- destructive
- unhealthy
- unethical
- competitive
- dishonest
- unforgiving
- untrusting
- jealous
- deceitful
- controlling
- unharmonious
- noncompassionate
- lonely
- unaccepting

The things that cause dysfunction in the home are the same things that jeopardize spirituality, which is about being connected. If you review the major classifications of mental illnesses—mood disorders (depression, bipolar disorder), anxiety disorders (panic disorder, obsessive-compulsive disorder, post-traumatic stress disorder), thought disorders (schizophrenia), and personality disorders (borderline, narcissistic, dependent)—you realize that all these disorders are really about a lack of connection and that the labels themselves tend to reinforce the disconnection of those people who are so labeled.

The starting point of all spirituality and of good mental health is being connected to self, to others, and to something bigger and greater than oneself. As lawyers working in a profession that is inherently adversarial, we are sitting ducks for the "disease" of disconnection. If you are going to jump out of an airplane, you need to carry a parachute. If you are going to be a lawyer with good mental health, you need to actively promote those activities that will keep you connected to self, to others, and to a larger purpose.

Andrew Young once said, "People don't change overnight and they never change because they are wrong, they change when they somehow become secure enough to want to do better." The healing begins whenever a person perceives that another person is listening and cares. The process of emotional healing, of being a person who builds up rather than tears down, is not easy, but it is the simple process of connection.

CHAPTER THIRTY-SIX

The Unhappiness Paradox

If We Have More, Then Why Are We Less Happy?

THE RICHER WE HAVE GROWN as a society, the more dissatisfied we have become.[1] Lawyers seem to share this unhappiness paradox, as much or more than any other group in our culture. Today we are part of a society where depression and anxiety disorders have reached epic proportions. Many people suffering from these conditions are not offered, or do not follow, an integrated treatment approach that addresses the mind, body, and spirit aspect of disease. The social stew we swim or live in (just like the microbes we breathe) plays a major role in determining whether we are healthy or sick. It is important to realize that the social conditioning of omnipresent ads, tawdry sex, and graphic violence tends to isolate us into individualistic self-centered consumers and pleasure seekers—just like the lawyer philosophy of "work hard, play hard."

To be healthy individuals—to recover from mental health disorders such as depression and anxiety—we need to build into our lives the social structures of family, friends, professional organizations, and religious and civic activities that support our common humanity. Without this life-enhancing social support, our normal cultural milieu creates conditions where prolonged hours of work, or the death of a loved one, may well push us into a medically defined illness called depression. Depression is a disabling and treatable disorder. However, we tend to view it differently from other diseases. Lawyers don't talk about "toughing it out" with their asthma. Instead they take medication that allows them to function so the disease state does not overwhelm them. This is equally important with depression. Pharmacological treatments for depression can give patients the chance to function at a more normal level so that they can address issues that might have triggered the condition, such as the need to fully grieve the loss of a loved one.

One of the peculiar aspects of depression is its subtlety. Like most chronic conditions, depression does not announce its arrival with any sort of acute pain or recognizable sign of illness. More often what happens is a sort of gradual slide into a state of despondency and low energy that appears clear only in retrospect to suggest the onset of a disease. Depression is an illness that can be effectively treated and managed, especially if it's treated early. Unfortunately, as lawyers, we don't want to consider that we might have a problem with depression, much less address it with early intervention and treatment.

Depression is a disease of isolation. Lawyers with depression tend to become defined in narrower and narrower routines until they can't return phone calls or even get out of bed in the morning and go to work. Unfortunately this isolation gets in the way of the social support and the exercise of those neuronal structures in the brain that deal with positive relationships that are the key to restoring a healthy brain chemistry balance. Not only is stabilization through pharmacological treatment important, so is the assistance of a good therapist who can help the patient understand the walls and barriers that have been built as survival mechanisms around the patient but now keep recovery and health out.

In 1901, Sir William Osler, a renowned physician of his time, said: "The way to live the longest is to acquire a chronic disease and take good care of it." Said another way, the way to live a long life is to learn early on how to heal from ailments. We live in a culture that promotes the illusion of happiness, and as lawyers, we work in a profession with attributes of power, prestige, and material well-being that are often seen as synonymous with happiness. These attributes, and much of our society's mores, are at best neutral. If we base our happiness on just these values, we will never have "enough" of these things and will never be truly happy. For many lawyers, getting to the "top" will not even be an option if depression sets in and is allowed to persist untreated.

Metaphorically, the idea of being pushed down by sadness or non-clinical depression is a way the psyche tells us to examine more closely what is going on in our lives—to look within. Are we meeting our physical, mental, emotional, and spiritual needs on a regular basis in a life-sustaining way? We each must find our own unique way to do this.

While the pain of a chronic disease is a sure way to force us to look at these issues, it is not the only way. We need not acquire a chronic disease to adopt the same realistic, objective way of looking at our lives that serious illness brings. As lawyers, we need to actively seek out the sort of relationships that foster well-being in our personal and professional lives, and at the first sign of trouble, reach out for help.

CHAPTER THIRTY-SEVEN

Feelings

How to Become Friends with Our Feelings

FEELINGS ARE BASIC to being human; they are how we interface with the world. We perceive the world through our five senses. We see, hear, taste, smell, and touch what is around us. Our feelings help us make emotional sense out of what we have perceived from these sensory perceptions. Feelings—what are they? How do they work? And how do they contribute to or distract from good mental health? Despite the fact that many of us lawyers would prefer to think we do not have any feelings, our experience of life is a feeling process.

Many mental disorders are based on something awry with our feeling process. We may be aware of uncomfortable feelings and repress them, or if we allow ourselves to feel them, we may feel overwhelmed by the experience. Either way, feelings are a sort of "weather radar" that tells us the state of our emotional health at any given time.

In order to experience good mental health, we must feel understood and accepted by others. Each individual needs to feel respected as an individual. We need to feel loved and respected to have healthy interpersonal relationships. The mechanism by which love and respect are relayed to the brain is through our feelings. If we want to be loved, we must reveal ourselves. We reveal ourselves through the feelings we express to others. As obvious as this may seem, we often go through life avoiding expressing our true feelings. There are many reasons for this. Most of these reasons have to do with self-protection. The fear is often "If I reveal myself to another, I will not be loved or respected."

The incongruence between how we present ourselves to others and how we actually feel can become a pattern of inauthenticity that disconnects us from ourselves. For example, if we profess to love when we are full of hostility, we are presenting not only a false front to others, but we are avoiding a true experience of ourselves. This state of disconnection or internal conflict induces stress, and our body's response is often to take energy from other activities in order to seek relief from stress.

Just as the failure to express our true feelings causes trouble, the failure to discipline our feelings, or their "overexpression," can also cause difficulties. The process of growth and maturity is not only one of learning how to authentically express our feelings, but also to do so in a way that takes responsibility for the expression of those emotions. In short, we can't let our emotions "run the show." The difficulty in trying to steer this middle path is that even with the people we care about the most, we may end up sharing very little of our true feelings, beliefs, or needs. Because we have such an inherent basic need to be loved, we fear the truth that may come with openness, and our natural inclination is to present the sort of person we believe would be accepted and loved, and to attempt to hide what does not conform to our internal image of how we *ought* to be.

Another reason that we may hide our feelings is because of our difficulty in handling change. Change has become so common in our modern life that this phenomenon is a serious impediment to our being able to authentically express our feelings. For many of us, change is frightening, and so to moderate the emotional impact of change on us, we try to see ourselves as constant. We internalize an image of ourselves in which we believe we are a certain way that is unchangeable, when in reality our needs, desires, goals, values, behaviors, and feelings change constantly with experience and age.

Perhaps the most important reason we don't show ourselves authentically to other people who are important to us is that we don't really know how. We often grow up learning, through our experiences with others, the ways to conceal our true identity. We are not taught how to reveal it. Our society teaches us, in fact probably pressures us, to suppress emotions and characteristics that are deemed socially unacceptable. Of course, this is an important lesson for interacting in a social setting. Too often, however, we take this lesson of what is appropriate or inappropriate in a social setting and apply it to all our intimate interactions with others. We don't learn how to be private just when we need to, and also to be honest and open when we wish without fear. The task before us, in all stages of our life, is to learn how to enjoy experiencing our feelings authentically, rather than having the feelings themselves create a mask that separates us from others.

We need to avoid suppression of our feelings and, at the same time, avoid acting out our feelings in an inappropriate way. We must do this while being open to the next feeling that will come along. This is the mechanism by which we experience our lives. Why do Americans enjoy going to the movies? Part of the enjoyment of the escape into the darkened theater is being able to experience our feelings vicariously through someone else. We are often afraid to reckon with the fact that we are the star in our own show, because with that starring role comes the responsibility to accept the wide variety of feelings that we have as we encounter life. Feelings are our internal reactions to our experiences. Our feelings may make us tremble, sweat, or have a surge of energy, because, although feelings are internal reactions, they have outward signs. Sadness is inside of us, but we may cry or frown on the outside. Anger is within us, but we may stare or shout at the person with whom we are angry. Feelings are always internal states, but they are states that are communicated to those around us.

Expressing feelings is difficult, particularly when there is a risk of being rejected or laughed at because of their expression. The more personal the feeling, the greater this risk we often feel in expressing the feeling. Individuals who grow up in alcoholic families or other dysfunctional family situations tend to be overly sensitive. These adult children of alcoholics often fear that others will judge them for expressing strong feelings.

Allowing ourselves to feel is the most natural and joyful part of being alive and being human. Feelings are what allow us to bond in our close relationships, as well as add meaning to the things we experience in the world. The authentic constructive expression of our feelings is one of the most important tasks of managing our relationships with others.

The starting point to healing is awareness. We can learn how to manage our feelings appropriately once we are aware of what they are. We can only express feelings that we acknowledge. We can't communicate feelings we refuse to accept as our own.

We imagine a person who is without feelings to be like a machine. Those people who enjoy life the most are probably those who have developed the full range of human emotions and feelings and have the least difficulty expressing them in a constructive fashion. Feelings of caring for another person, even feelings of anger toward another, are potentially highly rewarding experiences if they are authentically and constructively expressed.

We don't control our feelings. Feelings are an involuntary response to a mental or physical stimulus. Because they are involuntary, feelings are neither right nor wrong; they just are. However, I must be quick to add that what we do with our feelings—our actions in response to them, our expression of them—will be viewed by us and others as either right or wrong. Our actions, even including our faults and attitudes, do have a morality. The quality of their expression moves us more into being the authentic person that we truly are, or builds barriers in our lives to the experience of the person we truly are.

I often find that lawyers who are strong in their analytical abilities are weak in the perception of their own feelings. Sometimes a lawyer is very acute in sensing feelings of others but has very little awareness of his or her own feelings.

Here are some ways to help ascertain feelings:

- If the word "feel" is followed by the word "that," it is not a feeling, rather, it is an opinion or a thought. For example, in the statement "I feel that you tried that case well," the speaker is not expressing a feeling. He or she is instead expressing his or her opinion about how the listener tried a case.
- Similarly, if the word "feel" is followed by the word "like," it is probably not a feeling. For example, in the statement "I feel like you are wrong," the speaker is not expressing a feeling, but an opinion about the rightness of the listener's activity.
- If you can substitute the words "I think" for "I feel," then you are probably expressing an opinion or belief and not a feeling. If you can substitute a form of the verb "to be" for the word "feel" and it still makes sense, it is probably a feeling. For example, "I feel happy" can also be "I am happy." "I feel sad" can also be "I am sad."

In any conversation, many of us express our feelings nonverbally. Our words offer facts or information, but eye contact and other cues can communicate feelings about what we are saying. In order to learn to be more authentic in our lives—that is, more in touch with our true self and less stressed by acting out of an image of how we think we should be—it is important to become aware of whether our expressions of feelings are congruent with our true feelings. For example, in a conversation, are we smiling outwardly but actually gritting our teeth with resentment? As we develop more consciousness of how we feel, the awareness of repressed feelings will actually lighten our load.

The second task for learning to be more authentic in our lives is to become more aware of how we accept our feelings. We often suppress feelings because we don't like what we are feeling. The paradoxical fact is that acceptance of negative feelings is the key to allowing them to dissipate. Once they are accepted, much of the energy of the feelings often dissolves. When the feelings are not accepted, they tend to recycle over and over again, causing additional strife and uneasiness.

Once we become aware of our feelings and accept them, then there is the opportunity to enjoy them. If it is a positive emotion (joy or happiness), then the expression of that feeling to another person is what is often necessary to consummate the feeling and bring it to its natural conclusion. In other words, feelings may require that we take some action after we have become aware and accepted them. For example, if we see a beautiful sunset on a gorgeous fall day that causes us to feel joy, the action may be simply to mutter a prayer of thankfulness for the beauty of the day, or it may be to share the moment with a friend, or it may be to write a poem about the experience. Taking action on our authentic feelings makes us more at home with who we are as human beings.

If the feeling is a negative one, such as anger over being hurt by another, the process is similar. First, we need to become aware of the feeling so we do not mask it. And second, we need to accept the feeling. Acceptance is difficult because it may also include accepting that we are being overly sensitive, that we felt bad about something that was probably not intended to be a slight at all. And third, we need to take action. This may involve sharing with another person our vulnerability to being subject to the uncomfortable feeling. It may involve muttering a simple prayer asking that the feeling be removed. It may involve using the energy created by the negative feeling to constructively tell another person how we feel or to set a boundary. Or it may involve deciding to handle a situation differently in the future.

There are many types of destructive behaviors that can emerge from a feeling. Because of the discomfort caused by the feeling, we may engage in a behavior to make us feel different without ever being aware of or accepting the feeling. In this category are a whole range of behaviors that are precedent to addiction and depression. We may use an external chemical to make us feel different so that we don't have to experience the continuation of the negative feeling. We may repress the feeling and then become depressed. We may use sugar or caffeine to make us feel different so we don't have to deal with the difficult feeling.

Another destructive pattern of handling feelings is to act them out in an inappropriate way. We see this in road rage incidents where a person becomes upset and full of rage because another driver is simply not handling a vehicle the way he or she thinks this driver should. Road rage is often symptomatic of the fact that there are repressed feelings of anger or frustration that get triggered by the behavior of others with whom one has no relationship.

Ultimately feelings are the medium through which we experience life—the good, the bad, the ups, the downs. Feelings are also the vehicle by which we experience who we authentically are in this world. The bottom line is that we are stuck with them. Given this circumstance, we might as well learn to explore them, to become aware of them, and to accept them. Once we accept them, we can learn how to take actions in our life based on feelings to create the kind of life we would like to have, which makes us most authentically a part of this world.

CHAPTER THIRTY-EIGHT

Beethoven's Counterpoint

How to Thrive under Difficult Circumstances

A LITTLE OVER TWO HUNDRED YEARS AGO, in 1801, Ludwig van Beethoven was thirty-one years old. He was living in poverty, losing his hearing, wallowing in the depths of despair and hopelessness, and contemplating suicide. Twenty-three years later, utterly deaf, no longer suicidal, and infinitely creative, Beethoven composed the life-affirming, lyrical chords of his Ninth Symphony. What are the factors that allowed Beethoven's life to turn around, and could these factors help stressed-out lawyers struggling with addiction, depression, or other chronic illness? If we look backward in time, we can find some answers.

Beethoven did not suddenly switch from a life of helpless despair to a life of creative energy and joy. Beethoven was not what we would today call a paragon of good mental health. He never had the courage to tell others of his deafness. He remained an ordinary man with ordinary vulnerabilities and vanities. He visited a number of individuals who claimed they could cure deafness, but they offered no remedy. Despite these adversities, somehow Beethoven managed to thrive—to perceive his world with joy and gratefulness.

Psychologists, including Paul Pearsall, author of *The Beethoven Factor: The New Positive Psychology of Hardiness, Happiness, Healing, and Hope,* have looked at Beethoven's life and tried to identify the characteristics that allowed him, and others like him, whom they call "thrivers," to persevere, endure, and ultimately feel happy, despite physical ailments or other adversities.

Thrivers were found to have these three common characteristics:

1. Emotional openness: Thrivers embrace their emotions without resistance and let them flow naturally. Thrivers realize that challenging emotions such as fear, anger, and anxiety are not negative forces in their lives. These emotions only become negative forces when people allow themselves to become *stuck* in these ways of being in the world. Despite the challenging feelings of frustration and despair Beethoven experienced, he did not stay stuck. He experienced life deeply but was not attached to the feelings that came with the experiences.

2. Emotional detachment and curiosity: Thrivers are able to succeed because they seem to understand that challenging circumstances and the feelings that go with them are temporary. No emotion—happiness or grief—lasts forever. Thrivers seem to have an intuitive sense that life is made to experience. They don't focus on the pain of grief or anger, and they don't obsess about holding onto feelings of happiness and joy. They live by embracing all life's experiences and by avoiding becoming stuck on the emotional state related to the experience.

3. Ability to learn from misfortune: Thrivers seem to realize that suffering can be a transformative experience that makes them stronger. They know that experiencing the full range of human emotions is essential to living a truly authentic life.

One way thrivers adapt is through a sort of "psychological immunization." Emotional trauma, while devastating, can make us stronger. By going through difficult life experiences, we can experience a sort of emotional vaccination that can help us through future challenges. The key is to deal with the original trauma in a straightforward and forthright manner. Beethoven did this with his hearing disability. He tried to find a cure for his deafness, but when he couldn't find a cure, he didn't try to avoid his feelings of disappointment by taking pills or using alcohol or engaging in a destructive or obsessive behavior. Ultimately, going *through* the storm is what builds emotional resilience.

A second way thrivers adapt is by lowering their expectations. This has been a surprising find by those who have studied people who seem to thrive well. These thrivers don't develop emotional toughness or ways to rebound faster from a crisis, but they do develop ways to thrive by lowering expectations of both themselves and life. Thrivers do not have to be on a high of one success after another to feel good about life. They tend to have lower thresholds to experience joy and happiness in life and, in the process, are able to forgive themselves for their short-comings and not take personally the random harshness that they may encounter in the world.

In recovery terms, this is referred to as "accepting life on life's terms." It means maturing sufficiently to give up the feeling of entitlement that all children have. This is often difficult. We live in a modern world that encourages high expectations.

In a culture that often encourages us to say yes to more projects and ambitions, thrivers seem to be able to have less, do less, and say no when their happiness and health depends on it. The bottom line is that people do not thrive because they finally accomplished the impossible or overcame tremendous obstacles. They thrive because they remain engaged with their life and problems long enough to find meaning in them. People thrive because they look for and find wonder in the common everyday aspects of life.

A common characteristic of thrivers is their ability to mentally readjust their life to suit their current reality. Beethoven had to deal with the harsh reality of his deafness. He came to terms with this disability in a way that allowed him to achieve creative genius. The key to this is the conscious act of accommodating one's view of what he or she thinks life *should* be like to match the reality of current life at any given time. Thrivers seem to know when to create a consciousness of lowered expectations, if they must, and higher hopes when they realistically can.

When a crisis comes along, thrivers seem to know that their view of themselves and the world may be inadequate to address their current crisis. They are able to find a new consciousness of expectations that allows them to go forward. Thrivers like Beethoven know how to re-create their own view of themselves and the world, even when forces outside their control keep tearing their ideas down. This allows them to create their own place in the world. Ultimately their greatest creativity is their awareness of and ability to change their own consciousness.

Lawyers, as a group, often face the enduring strain of very high self-expectation in life and career that can cause high levels of stress which, in turn, challenges and tests their ability to thrive in adverse situations. A recent doctoral dissertation studied the relationship between stress, depression, work addiction, and attributional style among lawyers in North Carolina.[1] The study found that 27 percent of the lawyers surveyed were at risk for depression, 53 percent had pessimistic attributional styles, nearly 26 percent were work addicted, and 51 percent had elevated levels of perceived stress.

Through the years I've advised many stressed-out lawyers. Many of these lawyers share the same complaints. Peter, a thirty-one-year-old lawyer who works for a prestigious law firm, is married, has two children, and makes more than a $100,000 a year. He works sixty hours a week and tries to bill at least two thousand hours a year. He spends his precious free time thinking about things he has to do at the office and often wakes up early in the morning, unable to go back to sleep. By the time the weekend rolls around, he is too tired to engage in family activities. Peter is aware that his kids are growing up rapidly, but he feels hopeless about his ability to more actively participate in their lives. This lawyer excelled as a student, developed high expectations for himself, and was subject to high expectations from family members and others. How can lawyers like Peter learn to thrive despite these challenges? Amiram Elwork, in his book *Stress Management for Lawyers: How to Increase Personal and Professional Satisfaction in the Law*, offers three characteristics common in lawyers who thrive under stress:

1. Commitment. Lawyers with commitment have a personal sense of the value and meaning of their personal and professional lives.
2. Competency. Lawyers who believe they are competent are able to respond to issues in their life from a perspective that allows them to create positive change.
3. Goodwill. Lawyers of goodwill have a generally positive outlook and treat others with professional courtesy and respect.

Elwork's characteristics seem to be markers for good mental health during basically good times. During challenging times, stress is not always predictable, and as the recent survey cited on page 150 showed, the attributional style of most lawyers is not a positive one, but rather pessimistic. When external circumstances change in unpredictable ways, those who are able to thrive tend to be those who have the characteristics of a Beethoven. They are the individuals who are able to readjust their expectations and attitude so that they can thrive in the difficult reality in which they find themselves. Underlying the attitude of the thriver is an attitude of humility and gratitude for what he or she has (despite the difficulties reality may offer) and a willingness and desire to act on this awareness in a creative way in the world.

CHAPTER THIRTY-NINE

Good Mental Health and the Lawyer's Gift

What Is the Essential Nature of the Work
We Do As Lawyers?

The gift is to the giver, and comes back most to him—it cannot fail.
—Walt Whitman, "A Song of the Rolling Earth"

IN A 2004 SPEECH given at the University of Wyoming Fine Arts Center in Laramie, Wyoming, Supreme Court Justice Sandra Day O'Connor noted that job dissatisfaction among lawyers was widespread, profound, and growing. She added that attorneys are more than three times as likely to suffer from depression as nonlawyers and more apt to become dependent on drugs, get divorced, or contemplate suicide. Part of the problem, O'Connor believes, is the development of a "win at all costs" mentality that may mean a lawyer has to push the limits of ethics or morality to win the case. While Justice O'Connor's observation is not new, it is worth trying to ascertain what may lie beneath this remark.

I believe O'Connor is asking us to examine the nature of our professional services as lawyers. It is my premise that for a lawyer to be satisfied with his or her work, some of the work must be seen as a gift. Legal services exist in two economies, a market economy and what I would like to call a gift economy. At first glance it seems that only the market economy is essential, but the ultimate reality to preserving the profession may be the reverse. It is my opinion that law as a commodity can survive within the market, but without room for altruism in the legal services rendered, then the mental health that promotes professionalism in lawyers is diminished. Part of the dissatisfaction with the profession Justice O'Connor cites, comes from lawyers seeking to participate in a gift economy, but finding themselves confined to a market where law is practiced only as a commodity.

There are several distinct ideas about the nature of gift giving that lie behind the proposition I am suggesting. A gift is a thing that bears some human quality that makes it more than a commodity. A gift is something that is not simply acquired by an act of will. It is something that is bestowed by virtue of talent and by virtue of human relationship. Mozart composed on the harpsichord at the age of four—this was his gift. The great jurists of our American legal tradition, such as Marshall and Frankfurter, had gifts.

We know that the practice of law is just not simply a matter of logic. We rightly speak of a lawyer's intuition or inspiration as a gift. As a creative lawyer works, some portion of his or her creation is bestowed upon himself or herself—from his or her education, experience, and understanding, an idea comes into his or her head, such as a new way to address a problem or a new way to argue a legal theory. Most lawyers who are creative in their practice feel intuitively that some of what they are able to give their clients is a gift that is channeled through them. The intuition of this gift may not be as clear in the practice of law as it is in the field of art, whereof D. H. Lawrence said, "Not I, not I, but the wind that blows through me made this work." Still, there is something of the gift of inspiration that we feel, as lawyers, in the practice of our profession.

The challenge for lawyers, living in the economy of the market and the economy of the gift, is not to neglect the gift economy in both its inner and outer aspects.

The inner aspect involves the creative inspiration that allows us to thrive in the practice of law. The outer aspect is the sense of a gift given to our clients, to those for whom we provide services. Perhaps this is seen nowhere more forcefully than in the area of pro bono services. Justice O'Connor said, "Ensuring that there is equal justice under the law and not just for the wealthy, but also for the poor and the disadvantaged, is the sustenance that brings meaning and joy to a lawyer's professional life." O'Connor notes, being able to contribute legal services to those most in need is essential to keeping a strong foundation for our legal system. It is equally important for lawyers to see that part of the services we deliver to our paying clients is a gift. We pay a fee at the door of a museum or the entranceway to the concert hall, but when we are touched by a work of art or a piece of music, a gift comes to us that has nothing to do with the price paid. Similarly, for the client whose financial, emotional, and other difficulties have taken him or her into the lawyer's office, the empathy, understanding, and care given by the lawyer is a gift that positively affects both lawyer and client.

One of the things that many lawyers become aware of as they begin to value the gift found in the services that they deliver, is that a gift begets other gifts. Unlike the sale of a commodity, the giving of a gift tends to establish a relationship between the parties involved. In 1764, when Thomas Hutchinson wrote his history of the Massachusetts colony, he said, "An Indian gift is a proverbial expression signifying a present for which an equivalent return is expected." The term has survived today in the pejorative sense. Calling someone an "Indian giver" means that they are so uncivilized as to give a gift, while expecting a gift in return. The true meaning of the original expression was that a gift from a Native American was a gift that was to be passed on or reciprocated in some way. It contained the idea that gifts were energy that were not to be hoarded and were more than just commodities. Gifts were meant to increase in value as they were given over and over again. Christianity proposes a similar idea at Christmas. An individual may keep his or her Christmas present, but the sense of altruism is somewhat altered if you have not also given something back in return. This idea that a gift is something that is passed on—that it is more than just a commodity that may be stored—is needed to keep our profession from just being a commodity driven by the market economy.

In many myths and fairy tales, the idea of gifts is associated with fertility and abundance. Part of the reason for the traditional wedding feast is the showering of abundance on wedding guests as a way to initiate a cycle of plenty for the newly married couple. In other stories and folktales, such as the Northern Pacific culture's potlatch, the purpose of a gift-giving ceremony is to create harmony in a society. To be able to practice law with the idea that the services being rendered, while being in the market economy, are also a gift to create justice, is a way to provide harmony in our society. Harmony is not provided when the services given are simply a commodity.

Finding a balance between a pure market economy and a gift economy is problematic. The domination of either eventually brings forth its opposite. On the one hand, where there is no way to assert identity and an opportunity for private gain, we lose the benefit of the kind of freedom that brings innovation and individuality. On the other hand, where the market alone rules and where there is no piggybacking within a profession of the idea of a gift, then the traditional fruits to society of gift exchange are lost. Commerce then becomes associated with the fragmentation of community and the suppression of liveliness, fertility, and social feeling. If the legal profession does not contain within it the idea of a gift as part of the services provided, then there is a weakening of the vitality of the legal community itself.

The act of giving gifts can bring forth the full power of the creative lawyer. In the ancient world, the task of setting free one's gifts was a recognized labor. The Romans called a person's tutelary spirit *genius*. In Greece, it was called *daemon*. Socrates had a *daemon* that acted in his conscience; it would speak to him when he was about to do something against his true nature. In order to cultivate *genius*, it was necessary to provide gifts to it, often in the form of disciplines or sacrifices.

We can translate these ancient terms into more modern psychological terms. Today, we often describe the lawyer who is bent on exercising his own self-willed intellect and muscle as being narcissistic. This is the ego's road to depression. On the other hand, we see good psychological health in the successful lawyer who appreciates those he or she has learned from and been mentored by. The meaning of the gift is consistent in historical antiquity, modern psychology, and in traditional religious terms. To put it another way, whoever gratefully practices law and gives the gift of their genius and creativity along with the commodity of their services, will, by the act of giving of their services in this spirit, enter a sense of well-being with self and with their fellows and community. If this were more common, there might not be the job dissatisfaction, depression, or high rates of addiction found in lawyers. Ultimately, our dissatisfaction as lawyers may lie not in what we are not *getting* in life, but in what we are not *giving*.

CHAPTER FORTY

The Four Acknowledgments
Examining, Challenging, and Growing

ACKNOWLEDGMENTS are a form of willingness, of grasping new ways of being and deciding to live by them. My experience is that once acknowledgments are made, and actually lived, then everything from small meaningful change to significant change is possible.

The following four acknowledgments outline ways we examine, challenge, and grow in our lives.

Acknowledgment 1: I acknowledge that my life and my law practice are processes and not goals.

While goals can be helpful mile markers and invaluable planning tools along the road of life, it is easy to let these goals lose their value. We are then placed in the position of finding the next goal to direct our life toward. This first acknowledgment is about accepting that the process of moving toward any goal, in any direction, is more important than the goal itself. What does this acknowledgment about process bring to our life? It teaches us that the way we treat other lawyers when practicing law, the way we treat our clients, and the way we treat our family members and friends are in themselves the most important goals.

Acknowledgment 2: I acknowledge that the process is a matter of connections.

There are seven primary ways of connecting.

1. Connection with the self. This is the deepest level of connection within us. This connection goes beyond the internal ego

experience of our thoughts and feelings. Most people find that they need a process in their lives to strengthen this connection. Meditation and journaling are two practices that can strengthen the connection to self.

2. Connection with the body. Much material and scientific progress has been made because of our ability to analyze and break things down into their component parts. The reality is that many things operate organically as a whole—body, mind, and spirit. Our body is not separate from the rest of us. It is important to keep conscious connections to the body in order to assure good health. These connections may come through activities such as sports, yoga, dancing, woodworking, or other physical undertakings that we enjoy.

3. Connection with another. We need to be known by another on an intimate basis in order to know ourselves. Martin Buber called this an "I-Thou" relationship. This relationship allows us to see ourselves as who we really are—instead of through other's projections or our own fantasies. Being seen and acknowledged with clarity makes us feel more connected.

4. Connection with community. There are a number of layers of community. All are important, and at particular times in life, one layer may have more meaning than another. Generally, the layers of connection circle outward and become broader—church, synagogue, or sangha; local environmental groups; civic groups; local Bar section; local Bar committee; statewide Bar committee or section; statewide organizations; and national organizations. Each level of affiliation adds an extra dimension of connection to our community.

5. Connection with nature. Often the experience of nature is one of the most important spiritual connections a person has. Frank Lloyd Wright once said, "I believe in God, only I spell it nature." Another way to experience this connection with the natural world is through science. Researchers and professors in the area of physics and mathematics often have profound connections to the natural world through their work.

6. Connection with creativity. Most religious traditions hold creativity as an attribute of their God. To be most in touch

with this aspect of God is, for many people, to be immersed in their creativity. Creativity may be found in many areas, ranging from work as a lawyer to participating or observing more traditional creative arts such as painting, sculpture, photography, or dance. Many people connect with creativity through the appreciation of music, art, and theater. Often, artists who are really connected will refer to the experience of their creativity as a sense in which they are not *making* art, but that it is *channeled* through them.

7. Connection to God or a Higher Power. This connection loops us back to the first connection because without being connected to our inner self, it is very difficult to be connected to the Creator outside of our self. This connection can be strengthened through prayer, meditation, reading spiritual literature, or participating in a religious tradition.

Once we become aware of the seven primary ways we are connected, our task is to rebuild weak connections while looking for new avenues for connection. The more connected we are, the more we are in the process.

Acknowledgement 3: I acknowledge that living in the process means we acknowledge that truth, because it is always being revealed, is never complete.

This idea is connected to the old saying that the more strongly we feel about an idea, the less we probably know about it. This is particularly true of abstract ideas or ideas that seem universal. If we are trying to solve a problem of humankind, of war, of poverty, of natural disasters, we gravitate to big abstract ideas. Of course, these ideas are not any more effective in remedying the human condition than they would be in changing the nature of life.

Once we back away from global, abstract ideas, then we see that truth is always partial. The importance of this acknowledgement is to recognize that our own truth is incomplete and that there are many other people with different points of view that also have validity. This helps us be open to new careers, new ways of putting our law degree to work, and new ways to experience life. Accepting this new way of being can make it easier to rebound from difficult times, knowing that it is possible for good to come out of difficulty and that we don't always know best—our Higher Power might have other plans that will help us grow in our lives.

This acknowledgment helps us avoid the trap of the ego, which thinks it knows what is best at all times but may, in fact, be an impediment to our growth, maturity, and enjoyment of life.

Acknowledgment 4: I acknowledge that being in process means living in paradox.

Some of the most fundamental realities of human existence are paradoxes. Individuals do not achieve happiness by trying to be happy. Happiness is often a by-product of living an authentic life in which we serve something larger than ourselves. We need to strive for important goals, but know that the process of seeking to attain these goals is more important than the goals themselves. We need to learn to take life seriously, but at the same time wear it "like a loose garment." We need to take the risk of caring for and loving others deeply, while knowing that we all eventually depart from this life. We need to know that there are times when we need to be strong, and other times when we need to allow ourselves to be vulnerable—both enhance our experience, joy, and ultimate fulfillment in life. The greatest wound we have is often the source of our greatest gift. Our most challenging problem is often our greatest opportunity.

If we work to strengthen the connections described in the acknowledgments and concentrate on the process, we will transform the way we see our lives.

CHAPTER FORTY-ONE

Living on Purpose
Creating a Value-Driven Life

HOW MANY OF US conduct our day-to-day activities in a way that re-flects and reinforces our values? If I ask a group of lawyers to describe the things most important to them, many would perhaps say, "My fam-ily, my health, my relationship with God, and my creativity as a lawyer." If I ask them to describe what they do in a typical day, they might paint a picture of working long hours, overeating, neglecting regular exercise, and not spending enough quality time with their spouse and children.

When thinking about how we can keep our daily lives congruent with our values, I often think of the field of sports medicine. Tony Schwartz is a tennis player, a former *New York Times* reporter, and a writer who in the mid-1980s failed to live in accordance with what he valued most. Schwartz was offered the chance to cowrite a book with Donald Trump called *Trump: The Art of the Deal,* which became a best seller. After the book became a best seller, Schwartz felt empty despite success. He began meditating and studying psychics, philosophers, and healers. The result was a book published in 1995 called *What Really Matters: Searching for Wisdom in America.*

Schwartz interviewed a former tennis coach named Jim Loehr. Loehr had attended religious schools and then worked as a clinical psycholo-gist. Next, Loehr became director of a community mental health agency where he lost faith in therapy as a sufficient force to catalyze the kind of change people need, just as he had previously lost faith in religion as a means to help people deal with difficult life situations.

Eventually, Loehr became a sports psychologist. He found that con-ventional psychology's focus on emotional well-being did not focus enough attention toward physiological and spiritual well-being. In his practice, Loehr first addressed the issue of bodily energy—the need to throw out junk food and begin more healthy eating habits. Next, he began to listen to the kids at his tennis camps in order to discover how becoming a good tennis player could serve deeper values such as sportsmanship and courage, rather than serve a parent's ambitions, or one-upmanship, or fame.

In 1987, after studying hundreds of hours of videotape of professional tennis matches, Loehr made an interesting discovery. He found that during the fifteen- to twenty-second pauses between points, the less successful players dragged their rackets, muttered under their breath, and seemed distracted, looking around at the crowd. On the other hand, champions such as Chris Evert kept their heads high, even when they lost a point, and would concentrate their gazes on their racket or touch the strings with their fingers—in effect focusing and avoiding distraction.

Loehr had discovered the same process by which seventeenth-century monks achieved serenity in their daily lives. That is, automatic rituals keep people focused. After this discovery, Loehr went on to have an extremely successful career as a coach. He helped athletes develop rituals that addressed their individual weaknesses. Loehr's students eventually included Andre Agassi, Monica Seles, and Jim Courier, but by the early 1990s, Loehr began to lose interest in his current job. Part of the difficulty was that the tennis players he worked with seemed to operate in a social vacuum populated mainly by their own entourages, which were not accountable to any larger community. Loehr began to wonder how his method of coaching individual players could have a greater community impact—something greater than individuals pursuing their own self-interest.

At this time, Loehr ran into Schwartz, and they started work on a book that eventually was titled *The Power of Full Engagement*. This book used the wisdom Loehr gleaned from successful tennis players to help corporate workers maximize their energy under tight time demands. The case studies of the corporate men and women in the book could apply to the lives of many lawyers. Many of the participants had high blood pressure, were slightly overweight, worked long hours, and were too exhausted to exercise. After a distracted supper, they might spend another hour answering e-mails. Few practiced any "habits of the heart" to counterbalance the demands of their job. They were on task twenty-four hours a day, seven days a week. They didn't take the focused ritual breaks that Loehr had observed in successful tennis players. Instead, these men and women lived on blueberry muffins, candy bars, and sandwiches eaten at their desks. They worked too much, ate too much, and often drank too much. Running on empty, many lost touch with what they truly valued in their lives.

Loehr helped these individuals develop rituals that promoted their core values and, in the process, helped them pursue living with passion and enjoyment. He did this by designing rituals to help them create daily rhythms and rebuild physical energy. These rituals might include a walk in the park at lunch, a midmorning yoga break, a day a week working from home, a workout or snack in the afternoon. Then participants moved on to address emotional and ethical changes by performing writing exercises that asked questions such as, "What would you like written on your tombstone?"

A review of *The Power of Full Engagement* notes that Schwartz and Loehr's approach echoes the commonsense wisdom found in Twelve Step recovery programs—if you want to change the inside, change patterns of behavior on the outside. There is an echo of Aristotle in Loehr saying, "We are what we repeatedly do. Excellence isn't an act, but a habit."

The work of Schwartz and Loehr suggests that real change often comes from an understanding of and commitment to address bodily needs and spiritual needs as well as emotional needs. Repeating positive thoughts and patterns in our lives can leave positive patterns in our brain structure, just as repeated self-destructive thoughts and patterns leave us with negative patterns. We are physical animals as well as social beings, psychological beings, spiritual beings, and ritual beings. Therapeutic strategies have a greater chance of success when all these systems are mobilized in a systematic manner.

The work of Schwartz and Loehr reinforces what we know from practical experience—faced with destructive patterns in our lives, free will (or the neocortex) is of limited value. That is so because our destructive patterns operate out of the old reptilian brain—unaffected by thought strategies. What Loehr and Schwartz do is utilize the benefits of repetitive patterning on the reptilian brain to modify old behavior and encourage positive change. Rituals that encourage an early bedtime, daily exercise, a diet low in sugar, morning meditation, a ritual walk in the park, and reading inspirational literature can bring the kind of positive change that can make our way of life more congruent with our values.

Of course, it is hard to adopt new positive patterns. Here again, Schwartz and Loehr recognize the importance of group affiliation and effort. It is much easier to run if we have a running buddy. It is easier to achieve accountability for recovery if we attend a Twelve Step fellowship. What Schwartz and Loehr emphasize is that in order to impact the quality of our emotional life—that is, the emotional experience of how our life is lived—we need to greatly expand our understanding of the factors that go into creating that life. Growth begins with awareness—acknowledging that we don't control these factors directly. In fact, we control almost nothing directly, but we can help shape what shapes us. We can influence our life, even if we don't have direct control.

If we want to be effective and happy, we need to include on our list of values not just those things that we think about as being products of the will such as excellence and effort, but also self-acceptance, gratitude, and forgiveness. We need to practice daily rituals that allow us to have experiences of all these values and, most powerful of all, to act with other people on the values that serve causes greater than ourselves.

CHAPTER FORTY-TWO

Living Life's Questions

Writing Exercises to Illuminate Lawyers' Lives

LAST YEAR I HAD THE CHANCE to read two different biographies of John Adams. One was by David McCullough and was published in 2002. The other, by Catherine Drinker Bowen, was published in 1949. The stories were strikingly different because, although they were both written about the same man, each author took a different focus. McCullough's biography focused on Adams's emotional life—his insecurities and emotions under pressure—in a word, his psychology. Bowen, on the other hand, focused on the externals: what it was like for young John growing up in the aftermath of the French and Indian War, and the impact of the 1748 settlement of the War of Austrian Succession when King George II blithely returned to the French the territory the Massachusetts colony had gained at the cost of thousands of Massachusetts colonists' lives and fortunes.

McCullough's treatment reminds us that, unlike the period preceding World War II, we now live in an overwhelmingly psychological age. We see a merging of the personas of athletes, rock stars, and politicians by the media that reflects a fascination with the internal lives of others. This is in part a reflection of our own inability to look within.

There are good reasons we might not wish to look within. We may be tired of our culture's obsessive need to "psychologize" everything—to see an individual's actions as solely defined by his or her internal psychological makeup. A typical "nose-to-the-grindstone" lawyer is often caught up in the quest to establish and maintain an identity as a lawyer and never takes time to find out who he or she really is.

There is a middle way. A Zen phrase seems best to capture the process: "Know thyself, forget the self, see the opening of ten thousand things." While self-absorption is obviously not the goal, knowledge of the self is an essential part of the journey to a life of fulfillment and happiness. The unexamined life does continue to be the unlived life.

How do we begin this self-examination? One of the most fruitful processes or adjuncts to this process of self-examination is journaling. Journaling comes naturally for lawyers because we are drawn to the use of language, both oral and written. What makes journaling, or any creative process, exciting is that it is a journey into the unknown. It is a quest and record of the quest. The process itself is what opens and illuminates, more than the result. As author Rainer Maria Rilke said in *Letters to a Young Poet*, "Be patient toward all that is unsolved in your heart and try to love the questions themselves."

Journaling provides a process through which we gradually, without noticing it, begin to live our questions into answers. A happy and joyous life is about a life with meaning. Journaling provides a way to understand and to scale the barriers to freedom in our life and then to celebrate and to claim the meaning our life brings to this world.

Journaling often begins best by writing whatever comes into our head and then reflecting on what appears on the page. Difficult issues that have been repressed into the unconscious are most easily rediscovered in a context of trust and safety. To achieve a state of mind where we feel safe to write, we might remember a time when we had a client who really trusted us and spoke with us openly and honestly. We should write bravely and honestly, as if we are telling someone we trust about our situation. It may be helpful to simply sit down with pen and paper and write in a bound journal book or keep an ongoing journal file on the computer. Don't worry about spelling or punctuation, and don't edit or critique the writing. Just write.

The following journal exercises are a good starting point for any lawyer to begin the practice of honest self-examination.

Writing Exercise 1: As lawyers, we need to escape beyond our analytical mind, to become aware of negative messages we have internalized, and to tap into our creative nature.

Each morning, open your journal and write down whatever comes into your mind. Don't worry about the contents or if it makes sense. Write for ten or fifteen minutes without stopping, editing, or critiquing. This can be challenging for most lawyers who are conditioned to strive to make their writing clear and focused.

When writing in a journal, you may experience negative, self-judging voices that say, "I shouldn't write about this" or "That is stupid." Don't listen to this voice of censure. The secret to self-knowledge is to get past the ego stream of "shoulds" or "should-nots" and listen to what your life is really trying to say. Try to put down on paper what is below conscious awareness. When stuck, push ahead anyway. Thoreau said, "It takes two to tell the truth—one to speak, and one to hear." You must be your own best listener. Only by truly listening to yourself will you be able to write your way to a new level of self-discovery.

Writing Exercise 2: Writing details about the external world may open up internal discovery.

Choose something around you to write about. It might be the way an old law book is bound, the view out your window toward the court-house, or a favorite photo of your family. Be entirely present to what you are writing about. Sometimes this kind of writing is done most effectively when written as a poem. Don't write anything about yourself within the first twelve sentences.

If you write with great alertness and detail, you will discover something new about the thing you are writing about. As you reflect upon your observation, you will also discover something surprising about yourself.

If you feel stuck, give yourself time. One of the three prime characteristics of maturity is patience. Writing is a way to help you pause and be centered in your life, rather than being carried along on a vast current of e-mails, faxes, and cell-phone calls.

Writing Exercise 3: Thinking deeply about the activities we spend time on can deepen their meaning and help us achieve an internal state of serenity and gratitude.

Write about an everyday work activity in concrete detail. How does it feel to take a deposition, to defend a case, to draft a pleading? Does writing deeply about the activity give it a deeper level of meaning for you? In the process of writing about your activities and how you feel about those activities, you can come from one of two perspectives on your work life: blame or gratitude. You can wallow in the past as a source of all dissatisfaction and unhappiness, or you can reflect and understand it in a new, broader way. The cup is either half full or half empty. From a perspective of gratitude, your past can become whole.

Writing Exercise 4: Writing can help us each discover and understand our unique way of living in the world.

Identify legal mentors such as judges or other lawyers whom you respect. Identify legal institutions for which you are grateful. Write discerningly about your feelings of gratitude for what you have been able to experience because of these people or institutions.

Writing about the past, even with an attitude of gratitude, will often stir up ambivalence. You may remember both love and hate, acceptance and rejection. When you write through the division in your emotions about the past, you are getting close to healing. You are moving through a process where polarities can become paradox. For all of us, many of our internal troubles (and those of the external world also) come from taking half of a larger truth and beating ourselves, or others, over the head with it. Maturity and growth lies in the reconciliation of what seemingly cannot be reconciled, and then moving on.

Writing Exercise 5: Writing can help us understand and resolve the conflict that comes from facing hard ethical issues.

As a lawyer, you will eventually be confronted by an ethical dilemma. Don't run. Take a deep breath and spend time journaling about this dilemma and how it may reflect a serious inner conflict. The best choice may become clear. If not, try to move beyond the absolute language of "either this must happen or that must happen" and move toward understanding and writing down the feelings you have about the issue. Allow yourself to perform the rational analysis, but realize that the best decision may come from your deepest emotional core.

Writing Exercise 6: Inevitably, dream journaling will lead to discoveries. A dream is uniquely personal; only the dreamer has experienced its tone and affect, and only the dreamer can find meaning in a dream.

When you are aware of having a dream, write your dream down as soon as you awaken. Later that day, use what you remember about the dream as a starting point for further narrative or description. If you have a complex dream, befriend it and take the time to explore it fully.

Writing Exercise 7: The search for truth begins with asking the right question. As you explore your life by journaling, learn to think about the questions in your life that you are curious to answer.

Identify the important questions in your life right now and write them down. Don't obsess about finding the answer to the questions. For a week or longer, try to expand on each question, clarify and detail as precisely as possible what each question is—and then live the questions in your life and your writing by staying aware of them daily.

_____

_____

_____

_____

_____

_____

_____

_____

_____

_____

_____

_____

_____

_____

Writing Exercise 8: Just as important as using writing to reach into the unknown is using journaling to lift up those moments in your life when your consciousness was expanded, or when you experienced a reality that seemed greater than ordinary. Psychologists call these peak experiences.

Think back and remember moments when you felt a heightened awareness. Write down a description of what you remember and how you felt. It might be a time when you read a book that really inspired you, when you climbed a peak in the Rockies in time for sunrise, or when someone did something that overwhelmed you with gratitude.

Ask yourself where these moments occur in your work as a lawyer. Is there a pattern? Learn to write down descriptions of these peak experiences soon after they occur. Ask yourself what questions or answers these experiences bring. When you review this record of peak experiences, you will learn more about the way of being that is most pulling you into the world.

CHAPTER FORTY-THREE

Finding Happiness

The Paradox of How to Be Happy

*Happiness cannot be pursued; it must ensue as
the unintended side-effect of one's personal dedication
to a course greater than oneself.*
—Viktor E. Frankl

THE *NEW YORK TIMES* ran an article on September 7, 2003, that quoted Professor Daniel Gilbert's studies on happiness in humans. If Gilbert is right, then we are wrong to believe that a new car will make us as happy as we think it will. In the same way, we are also wrong to believe that winning that big case will make us as happy for as long as we might imagine. On the other hand, if Gilbert is right, you are also wrong to think that you will be more unhappy with a single setback, such as a broken wrist or broken heart, than with a lesser but more chronic problem such as a trick knee or a tense marriage. You are wrong to expect that the untimely death of someone in your family will leave you bereft for year after year.

The bottom line is that we are often not accurate in our predictions of how we will feel in the future, according to studies on happiness by Harvard Psychology Professor Daniel Gilbert, University of Virginia Psychologist Tim Wilson, Carnegie-Mellon Economist George Loewenstein, and Princeton Psychologist and Nobel Laureate in Economics Daniel Kahneman.

These four scholars have conducted a series of experiments about the decision-making process that shapes our sense of well-being. In their view, one of the critical steps in assessing well-being lies in understanding our emotional expectations about whether something will make us happy or unhappy.

According to their research, most of the actions we take—even big decisions such as to buy a house, have children, or work eighty hours a week for a fatter paycheck—are based on our internal and usually unconscious predictions of the emotional consequences of these events. What these social researchers have discovered is that while we get the big picture right—we know we will enjoy going to the theater more than going to the dentist—we tend to overestimate the emotional payoff in both the intensity and duration of future events. In other words, we might believe that making partner, getting married, or buying a new house will make life nearly perfect, but, almost certainly, the emotional satisfaction derived from these experiences will be less intense and of shorter duration than our emotional anticipation of the experience has predicted.

Similarly, Gilbert and his colleagues found that the impact of a negative life experience will also be less intense and more transient than test participants predicted. Gilbert sums this up by recasting the Rolling Stones' expression "You can't always get what you want" as "You can't always know what you want." In Loewenstein's view of their research, "Happiness is a signal that our brains use to motivate us to do certain things. And in the same way that our eye adapts to different levels of illumination, we're designed to kind of go back to the happiness set point. Our brains are not trying to be happy. Our brains are trying to regulate us." These researchers believe the tendency toward adaptation explains the gap between what we predict and what we ultimately experience.

This research is significant for lawyers because as a group we tend to be goal-oriented. We invest enormous amounts of energy in serving our clients. This research on happiness suggests that because of the adaptation process, happiness is not nearly as dependent on our goals as on the manner in which we work toward them.

Here is another way to look at the puzzle of happiness. Make a list of all the things that are most important to your happiness. Your list might include your children, spouse, faith in God, physical health, intelligence, and at least a certain amount of economic security. If you study your list for a while, it may become apparent how little control you have over the things you define as being important to your happiness. You may love your spouse and children but you have no control over whether that love will be returned or whether their health will endure. You may also discern that while you can enjoy habits that are good for your physical and mental health, you have no way to control the occurrence of cancer, heart attack, or disability from an accident.

Happiness seems to be more a product of our attitude: whether we see the objects of happiness as things we should *have* (entitlements) or as *gifts*. Ultimately, an attitude of gratitude for what is present, rather than feelings of deprivation for what is absent, seems to be the key to enjoying life.

Fundamental to gratitude is a kind of humility that encourages acceptance of our own fundamental limitations. The legal culture often does not encourage this. Rather it teaches that our value as human beings depends on what we can do, what we possess, whom we know, or how we look. These underlying cultural messages contribute to an attitude of selfishness and self-inflation that undercuts acceptance and gratitude.

While we all want to be happy, most strategies to compensate for the need to be happy usually mask feelings of inner fear and shame or of not living up to an invented image we have created. These strategies include absorbing ourselves in TV, junk food, gambling, alcohol, drugs, relationships, or sex. The more we use these strategies to try to feel good (or later to avoid feeling emotional pain) the more of a barrier they will be to the experience of happiness.

We use these strategies as devices to avoid experiences of challenging emotions, especially when these experiences are different from the way we *think* they should be. Gilbert and colleagues found that the gap between what we expect and our actual experience reinforces what we intuitively know—that all our efforts to obtain happiness through achievements and addictions will be short-lived at best. We may intuitively grasp the idea that genuine solutions can only come from acceptance and gratitude for the many things that give life meaning—most of which we cannot control. However, without something else to replace this old way of being, the old emotional controlling strategies will carry the day.

Much disease comes from trying to control our own happiness rather than being in a process of happiness. Fundamental to the process of happiness (as opposed to the goal of happiness) is acceptance of the current reality of our lives. The hardest part of acceptance is acknowledging that some troubling aspect of our life cannot be changed. For example, if I have a seemingly incurable health problem, live with a depressed family member, or have a child with a serious alcohol problem, such a circumstance is going to be difficult to bear. But if, in addition, I am also bitter, resentful, and angry about the problem, I have added another, perhaps worse, problem—a negative, judgmental attitude that will aggravate the issue and add fuel to the fire of resentment. The paradox for us as lawyers is to be able to fight passionately against injustice and unfairness, but at the same time accept that there is unfairness and injustice in the world that is beyond our control.

With emotional acceptance of this paradox comes gratitude. A profound sense of gratitude comes in appreciation of the things that bring happiness when we realize—not just intellectually, but on a deep emotional level—that one really has no control over the things that bring happiness.

Happiness comes when we let go of all the things we think we need to become satisfied. If we get these things, after some momentary exhilaration at having them, they will often no longer make us happy anyway. When we let go of both the things we think we need to be happy, and the negative coping strategies we have developed as a result of not having these things, then we can really be present to enjoy and appreciate what is occurring in our lives. We become happy by the manner in which we engage in life, not because of what we expect life to bring.

Notes

Chapter 1: Personality, Environment, and Addiction

1. "Addicted Lawyers Can Overcome Barriers to Recovery," *Alive & Free* (July 26, 2004), http://www.hazelden.org/servlet/hazelden/cms/ptt/hazl_alive_and_free.html?sh=t&sf=t&page_id=28949.

Chapter 2: The Addictive Personality

1. Paul Tieger and Barbara Barron-Tieger, *Do What You Are* (New York: Little, Brown & Company, 2001).

Chapter 5: Joe's Brain

1. A. Thomas McLellan and others, "Drug Dependence, A Chronic Medical Illness: Implications for Treatment, Insurance, and Outcomes Evaluation," *Journal of the American Medical Association* 284, no. 13 (October 4, 2000). Available online at http://www.uclaisap.org/AddClinic/documents/PDFs/2006/Drug%20Dependence%20as%20Chronic%20Illness.pdf.

Chapter 6: Self-Deceptive Thinking

1. Charles V. Ford, *Lies! Lies!! Lies!!! The Psychology of Deceit* (Arlington, VA: American Psychiatric Publishing, 1999).

Chapter 9: AA and the Establishment Clause

1. Derek P. Apanovitch, "Religion and Rehabilitation: The Requisition of God by the State," *Duke Law Journal* 47: 785–852.

Chapter 11: Codependency and Addiction

1. Sharon Wegscheider-Cruse, *Another Chance: Hope and Health for the Alcoholic Family,* 2nd ed. (Palo Alto, CA: Science and Behavior Books, 1989).

Chapter 14: Alcoholism in Older Adults

1. U.S. Department of Health and Human Services and U.S. Department of Agriculture, *Dietary Guidelines for Americans, 2005,* 6th ed. (Washington, D.C.: U.S. Government Printing Office, January 2005). Available online at http://www.healthierus.gov/dietaryguidelines.

Chapter 15: Compulsive Gambling

1. Chad Hills, "The National Gambling Impact Study Commission (NGISC) Report: What Does It Mean? What Does It Say?" *CitizenLink.org* (November 26, 2003), http://www.family.org/cforum/fosi/gambling/gitus/a0028977.cfm.

2. J. Welte, G. Barnes, W. Wieczorek, M. C. Tidwell, and J. Parker, "Alcohol and Gambling Pathology among U.S. Adults: Prevalence, Demographic Patterns and Comorbidity," *Journal of Studies on Alcohol* 62 (2001): 706–12.

Chapter 16: Cocaine

1. Substance Abuse and Mental Health Services Administration, *Overview of Findings from the 2004 National Survey on Drug Use and Health* (Rockville, MD: Office of Applied Studies, 2005, NSDUH Series H-27, DHHS Publication No. SMA 05-4061). Available online at oas.samhsa.gov/nsduhLatest.htm.

2. Substance Abuse and Mental Health Services Administration, *Results from the 2004 National Survey on Drug Use and Health: National Findings* (Rockville, MD: Office of Applied Studies, 2005, NSDUH Series H-28, DHHS Publication No. SMA 05-4062). Available online at oas.samhsa.gov/nsduh/2k4nsduh/2k4Results/2k4Results.htm.

Chapter 18: Preventing Suicide in Lawyers

1. E. G. Krug, K. E. Powell, and L. L. Dahlberg, "Firearm-Related Deaths in the United States and 35 Other High- and Upper-Middle-Income Countries," *International Journal of Epidemiology* 27 (1998): 214–21.

2. Patrick J. Schiltz, "On Being a Happy, Healthy, and Ethical Member of an Unhappy, Unhealthy, and Unethical Profession," *Vanderbilt Law Review* 871, no. 52: 879–80.

Chapter 20: Beyond Relief

1. David D. Burns, *The Feeling Good Handbook* (New York: Penguin, 1999).

2. National Institute of Mental Health, *Older Adults: Depression and Suicide Facts*, revised (May 2003, Publication No. 03-4593). Available online at http://www.nimh.nih.gov/publicat/elderlydepsuicide.cfm.

Chapter 22: Attitude and Disease

1. David Spiegel, Sandra E. Sephton, Abba I. Terr, and Daniel P. Stites, "Effects of Psychosocial Treatment in Prolonging Cancer Survival May Be Mediated by Neuroimmune Pathways," *Annals of the New York Academy of Sciences* 840 (May 1998).

Chapter 27: Stuck

1. Don Peck and Ross Douthat, "Does Money Buy Happiness?" *Atlantic Monthly* 291, no. 1 (January/February 2003).

Chapter 36: The Unhappiness Paradox

1. L. Becchetti and M. Santoro, "The Wealth-Unhappiness Paradox: A Relational Goods/Baumol Disease Explanation," in *Handbook of Happiness in Economics* (May 2004).

Chapter 38: Beethoven's Counterpoint

1. Mary H. Howerton, "The Relationship of Attributional Style, Work Addiction, Perceived Stress and Alcohol Abuse in Lawyers in North Carolina" (Ph.D. diss., University of North Carolina at Charlotte, 2004).

About the Author

Since 1994, **DON CARROLL** has been the director of the North Carolina Lawyer Assistance Program and its predecessor program, Positive Action for Lawyers (PALS). He is a certified employee assistance professional and is licensed in North Carolina as an employee assistance professional. Don currently chairs the Board of the Chemical Dependency Center, a nonprofit prevention and outpatient treatment agency serving the Charlotte, North Carolina, community. His regular columns about the Lawyer Assistance Program have appeared in the *North Carolina State Bar Journal* and the *Campbell Law Observer*.

From 2001 to 2004, Carroll served on the American Bar Association's Commission on Lawyer Assistance Programs. He currently serves on the Commission's Advisory Board. In 2000, Don received the Addiction Professionals of North Carolina Outstanding Achievement Award for his work as director of the North Carolina Lawyer Assistance Program. That same year he also served on the planning committee for the ABA's Commission on Lawyer Assistance Programs National Workshop.

Carroll served as a law clerk for the Honorable James B. McMillan, United States district judge for the western district of North Carolina. Carroll practiced civil litigation from 1975 to 1990 as an associate and partner with the firm of Helms, Mulliss, and Johnston; he then served as partner with its successor firm, Smith, Helms, Mulliss, and Moore.

Carroll received his law degree with honors from the University of Virginia in 1971. He holds a master of fine arts degree in writing from Vermont College and a master of philosophy degree from the University of Dundee in Scotland. Carroll received his undergraduate degree from Davidson College in 1967.

Carroll lives in Davidson, North Carolina. He has two children.